RENAISSANCE 2.0

RENAISSANCE 2.0

BUILDING A FUTURE ON THE LOVE OF OUR CHILDREN

ROB JEFFERIES

Rob Jefferies & Associates Pty Ltd

A catalogue record for this book is available from the National Library of Australia

Contents

Preface

Our children, our grandchildren... our inspiration!

Dear Lucy, Flora, Sunny, and Rose

The 20th of July 2019, the 50th Anniversary of the Apollo II landing on the moon, was the date that I knew I must start typing these words to you, Lucy, Flora, 'baby to be' Webb and the children of our children to come. Baby Webb was due in about six weeks and affectionately known as *'Cob'(Child on Board)* Webb.

50 years prior to the day, incredibly brave men made an unbelievable achievement, with the support of a united, highly expert team of scientists, engineers, managers and dedicated workers, but also with the support of the whole world, and first stepped on the Moon. They looked back at the Earth and saw this amazingly beautiful and tranquil blue planet in its orbit around the Sun. Standing there in a fixed orbit around the Earth, were they aware that they were at just the right distance from Earth to be part of the heavenly mass pulling on the world's oceans as it moved on its course around our planet; shifting the tides in and out, shaping the ebb and flow of the life of our marine plants and animals in different ways, acting on the atmosphere too? Over that great distance we were still connected.

Certainly, the absolute beauty of planet Earth, its place and scale in the infinite Universe, struck astronauts Neil Armstrong and Buzz Aldren as a life-changing experience; the first to take in this unique perspective of our world.

The Earth moving around the Sun at just the right orbit and distance so that we can exist, plants and animals flourish and the seasons that control when things grow and when they seed and die....... all in perfect balance.

Lucy, in your Year 2 at school you already knew a lot about the atmosphere, climate, the environment and how we must respect it, must recycle, and make sure we don't do harm to our world, nor to each other.

Could you imagine if our family grew up on the Moon! We would need water to drink and air to breathe, the surface is all dust, and we would need to find ways to make plants grow, maybe to breed animals too! Just think how every tiny drop of water and mouthful of clean air would be so precious. How every plant that grew would be a wonder and small miracle when it popped up from the fluffy moon-dust. We would have to contain all the air and water; controlled so it didn't drift off, because we couldn't live without it. Our whole life would be living in pods, capsules and space suits to contain life-giving oxygen and moisture we need, and to protect us from the desolate environment of the Moon.

Then, if we looked up at this incredible blue planet that had unbelievable amounts of water that would support billions of people, soils to grow all the plants we would ever need to feed them all, plus every kind of animal we could think of, we would wish to be right there.

If we lived our lives on the Moon, could we ever understand how the people on that beautiful blue planet allowed the oceans to start filling with the rubbish and plastic that they threw into it, so much that it was found in the fish that they ate and began to kill off the wonderful life those waters hold? Could we understand how the planet's communities expanded factories and power stations and chose to live their lives in ways that polluted the air they breathed, so in cities it choked and killed their own people, especially the sick, elderly or very young?

It would be inconceivable then for us to imagine it could be even worse, that the sheer volume of the gases produced by all those power plants, industries and activities would be allowed to pour into the atmosphere, so much that it would heat up and the weather systems would change, and with that, the world's environment and everyone and every living thing in it harmed in some way.

So, these words are for you Lucy, Flora, Sunny, Rose, and for all the children of our children, and others who may share concern for the changes happening now, and how it affects lives long into the future. Those who feel compelled to act now to try to change this. We live in a world that has all the resources and creative capabilities to provide an amazing environment and society for you and the children of generations to come.

The major threats to your future existence: massive damaging climatic change, ever widening gaps in financial capacity, political oppression and wars, need not exist. In fact, we should be making social and environmental change that offers enormous promise and enhanced living. These changes I have called *Renaissance 2.0*, reflecting a direct challenge to society's continued adoption of ever-evolving financial and industrial models to shape its future.

All around the world, we see evidence that human activities are harming our world... and your futures. Governments are starting to acknowledge this multiple-layered threat. Scientists are warning of catastrophic impacts on the environment and the world's population if swift action is not taken to address these threats.

The year 2050 has been set for achievement of many of the world's environmental targets and it is my hope that at that time, you will be able to look back, safe in the knowledge that people, communities, governments and countries have come together in building a world where social wellbeing, the environment and economic endeavour are in balance.

Why It All Means So Much

You are all so very precious to us and won our hearts from the very first moment our lives connected. Our life journeys became shared experiences, from the day of your births; or even earlier in the excitement and anticipation we felt prior to the birth of Sunny and baby Rose. But the moment that stays in my mind is the first time each of you looked straight into my eyes, to the depths of my soul, with your dark baby eyes which said to me, *"I know you and that you are here for me"*. Connection you share with your mums and dads, uncles and aunties; connection as we started our journeys together and a special privilege that mums, dads, grandparents and great grandparents across the world and throughout our human history are privileged to share.

In 2050, our journey together, dear Lucy, Flora, Sunny, Rose and children, is likely due to end; Nanna Jill and I will be 95 in July of that year and if we haven't already gone to live with God, we will be very ready to do so.

I have kept three things in mind as commitments to you as I go forward in writing the selections of thoughts and messages that have come together in this book to you:

- To be as honest and open as I can be.
- Look at what is happening in the world as I see it and consider where that may lead, and
- Acknowledge scientific realities, but in doing so seek ongoing spiritual guidance as I look for solutions and ideas, ideas that I believe will positively contribute to a better future and to help meet the challenges facing humanity.

I feel that is the very least that you are entitled to!

This book shares why we must change our way of life and business, what can be ours if we do so, and approaches that can be adopted by us as individuals, communities, organisations and countries to achieve the safe, sustainable and harmonious way of life we would want for our future generations.

The planet Earth is an amazing creation – and there is a future for it and for us – a future that holds promises of prosperity, harmony, environmental sustainability and beauty, and it is all within our grasp if the world community of today is prepared to unify in its pursuit.

Indeed, people do not need to feel overwhelmed by the global challenges before us; there are solutions available. However, changing our habits and lifestyles is always hard, even if for good reason. Even with the dire consequences of inaction, the question before us remains:

If we have a pathway to a sustainable future set out before us, will we come together in unity to take that journey?

1

Our Legacy: Your World

Every day involves an investment in a precious resource... your lives! It is
incumbent on us to use these days wisely.

On the 20th of July 1969, the Apollo 11 astronauts were connected from the starry outpost of the Moon to Earth, not only by the physical reality of gravitational force, but by the spiritual and emotional bonds of goodwill, concern and communal bond with everyone who shared the moon landing experience that day. Similarly, we are connected to each other, and through time, to future generations of children; through the earth we walk on and our spiritual, family and communal love and concern. The quality of life and well-being of children of the future will be directly linked to the actions we take as individuals today, as well as in the course of the journey we share between now and scientists' predicted time of reckoning in 2050.

Even if people agree that the way of life we lead is not sustainable, for most it seems an impossible task to alter the course that is set by powerful economies, government direction and a system of social and economic existence that has prevailed for centuries. Each of us are, after all, just one of over 8 billion people who exist on the Earth, how could we even contemplate taking on the massive scale of change that is required?

Let's consider what one small step did.

When 2 astronauts added their relatively small mass to that of the moon, the change in gravitational pull on the Earth was minuscule, but real change occurred in the way people of Earth came to view themselves as a community. People back then had a new perspective on humanity's place in the universe and the amazing things that can be achieved when people work to shared causes for common good.

Who Will Lead Us?

There is a growing tide of people, organisations, businesses and governments responding to the physical, social, economic and environmental challenges before us. Yet, there is still not enough unity in commitment and direction to expect that we are going to preserve all that people value today and all we enjoy in our physical environment. Nor can we expect to easily deliver the degree of health and well-being for future generations that should rightly exist. However, the momentum grows every day.

Scientists are saying that there is hope and opportunity to make things right, but the time to act must be now. With every year that passes it gets a whole lot harder; the window of opportunity to act is closing.

"The ultimate test of (a person's) conscience may be (their) willingness to sacrifice something today for future generations whose words of thanks will not be heard." - Senator Gaylord Nelson

Leaders of business and government organisations speak of taking a 'helicopter view' of issues, opportunities and challenges before them, stepping outside their operational activities and seeing a bigger view of the industry/organisational context. The best organisations do that as a part of how they plan, operate, and succeed in highly competitive situations. But that isn't enough anymore if the very world we all live in can no longer sustain our activities. A new way of thinking and acting is needed.

We need to move from a 'helicopter view' of our organisations in an industry to a 'lunar standpoint', considering our entire activities within the Earth on which we exist. Where we recognise that each of us and every organisation, company, region and country all have a part to play. All have an impact, good and bad, on this blue planet we live upon.

Throughout history, people have turned to leaders, government and business to chart the course for our communal future. Business, government, the large community-driven organisations, the scientific community itself are all aware of the issues and challenges we face, but still there is no adopted collective plan and insufficient action. The warnings are clear that too little is being done too late...

Why and how can this be? All the evidence is sitting before us!

There are many reasons, probably none of these are very good ones, and it will make no sense from a 'lunar view' of the world nor to our grandchildren in the age of 2050.

The Climatic Context

Sadly, scientists today believe that by 2050 there will be catastrophic impacts and the world's landscape devastated, unless we make substantial changes today. We must keep working to cut down the gases that pollute the Earth's atmosphere and cause its temperatures to increase.

We don't really know what that would look like, but we can surmise from current weather changes. Some areas are seeing record hot temperatures, stronger storms, cyclones and hurricanes, heat domes, fierce bushfires, longer periods of drought, and record floods now. However, because droughts, floods and fires have always been around at some level and we all want to live in the hope that nothing will change, many people still try to convince themselves that we can continue as things are.

The records show the world's temperature overall is increasing and more than that, now we are seeing undeniable losses in plant and animal species that are gone forever. We are seeing reduction in the water stored in the ground and in dams, and patterns of change in plant and animal species in the landscape and in the seas, including extinction.

Local and Regional Context

If the years pass without action, try not to be angry with the people of this and earlier generations. Uncertainty frightens people, and there are still political and corporate leaders who are telling us the change is not here and now or as bad as it is being portrayed; that we can wait longer, and we need to put today's economy first. If I walk outside today, all I see is just another beautiful sunny day, with the hills green, ospreys in the air and pelicans swimming in the river below our house. So, I can understand why so many people can't comprehend the scale of impending change, which is mostly subtle, gradual and silent in the World we live in now.

In the Geraldton area of Western Australia, we have a wonderful natural environment and landscape that supports strong fishing and agricultural industries. These are very diverse, with crayfishing, fishing, pearl farming and aquaculture; broad-acre crop farming, fruits and vegetables grown locally. Further out in the region to the north and east are pastoral activities, including sheep, goats and some cattle, and these fit better with that drier and sparsely vegetated country. Many visitors come because of the natural beauty of the place and its history, especially around August/September each year, to see the magnificent wildflowers come into bloom across the hinterland.

This area has already experienced an increase in average temperature and reduced winter rainfall[1]. If we try to imagine what these drier conditions will mean to the landscape where we live, I suggest we look at that of about 150 km or so to the northeast. Drier, a lot more barren, with stunted and sparse vegetation. With a drier climate and less water to draw upon for commercial uses, the activities dependent upon climate, soils and water supplies are likely to significantly change.

We cannot expect that the shift in our landscape to subtly transition to a more sparsely vegetated one, either. The impacts of droughts, windstorms, bushfires and heat are likely to create major dust storms that strip the very soil from the land and dump it into the sea or shift it in dunes that careen across the land. It may be decades or longer before things stabilise – and that assumes the climate doesn't continue to change.

Many areas of the world are starting to experience these changes now, especially where they do not have the resources or knowledge to revegetate and stabilise the soils. This has created huge, bare tracts of land that look more like they belong on the desolate landscape of the Moon than part of our watery blue planet. But it is not just increased droughts we are seeing now; rather, there are massive swings in weather patterns – from record floods in some years to heat waves and drought in others. This happens because the atmosphere seems to shift through extremes in its response to the increased thermal energy it now holds.

Through flow-on effects of climate change, adverse outcomes for natural and agricultural bio-systems arise, which may have catastrophic impacts on local communities. Charity organisation CARE reports[2,3] on the Somalia hunger crisis, impacting an estimated 7.8 million people, provides a stark illustration of these effects. These are the type of impacts we can expect to see more broadly across the globe.

Political & Industry Context

In democratic countries, political leaders are elected when what they say sounds good to the majority of the people who vote. As voters, **we** must accept blame for not wanting to hear what is difficult to deal with and accept, and **they** need to take responsibility for not coming together on the major issues and having agreed plans and policies that are based on the realities we all face.

In a broad sense, the systems and assumptions on which industry is based have served community well. Food, goods and services that we need or want are made affordable by competition and new technologies that drive costs lower. Businesses and governments employ a lot of people, but the drive to lower costs is very strong in these times, leading to cuts in jobs and services to people. For instance, Australia's major banks have pursued a program of automation, with each cutting hundreds of jobs over the past year.[4] While profitability of the banks may improve, there are detrimental societal outcomes; not only in people losing their jobs but impacts on customers too. Bank branches closing in rural communities affects business and local customers, and undermines the town's economy in the process.

In Australia, recent Royal Commissions into our most trusted corporate entities, our largest four banks, holding millions of Australians' savings and lending, found they had disgracefully abused their roles and the trust given by their customers, with false charges applied, bills to deceased people, and misleading practices. Whether it is through automation of processes, poor management cultures, or pursuit of cost cutting, if processes and the interface with employees, customers and affected community members are not ethically managed, then society pays a price. A price that could be avoided with forethought and consideration.

Changing the Agenda

The most significant way people are informed and shape their views today is through social media, and this has many positive aspects. However, technologies are being applied to the major social media systems in ways that don't just allow people to share and read but rather work to manipulate their opinions for personal, political or commercial advantage. Systems have been introduced that 'mine' personal data, then target and leverage prejudices, conveying inaccurate information. Wealthy and powerful people and organisations use data-driven advertising and psychological techniques to influence thinking. They use their influence to swamp people on social media with their viewpoints, their advertising and campaigns so they can wash over bad practices, get themselves elected, create personal or company profit, or give a false image of their actions or inactions.

While others are trying to influence or tell us how to think, look, or what to buy, many of us are becoming so personally invested in social media that it is insidiously shaping our thoughts, feelings and personalities. Not only can this affect how we think of ourselves, but it has an influence on our attitudes, which can flow to politics and directions in life.

The danger is that our emotional resilience leaves our own control and falls to the vagaries of what people or posts dictate through the social media platforms.

We need to be more than our social media persona. Social media is a tool for communication, not who we are.

Living in this kind of echo chamber can also lead to despair. We should not allow ourselves to despair when faced with the negative challenges of our world, although we do need to acknowledge the reality that current systems and thinking must change and evolve if the children of today and tomorrow are to have a quality of life that they all deserve to enjoy.

Each of us has a right to breathe clean air, have good health, and to strive to our potential, and with that comes a responsibility to ensure our success is not at the cost of the fundamental rights of others, not now nor in the future. To make sure we preserve such rights, we need new thinking and to reshape our way of doing things. This needs to come from you and I, the everyday people of this world.

People with a desire for a better society and safe, healthy environment in which to live need to set the new agenda. If not us, who will it come from, and why would we think government and corporate businesses will act without the community driving the changes required?

2

Dear Lucy

Be the wonderful person you were created to be.

You are such a bright and clever girl. I have known this from the day that your little hand reached out and wrapped tiny, chubby little fingers around the index finger of my hand; what were you, maybe three days old? As you grew into a toddler I thought, *now this young lady is one bright little possum and will be able to have any career she wants.*

Later, when only seven, it blew me away when I learnt you love designing rooms and buildings to live in, and instead of watching 'kids' shows', you tuned the TV into *House Rules* at any opportunity, to learn more about house design and renovation. The world is going to need clever designers and architects to provide homes, buildings, and safe built environments for people, in whatever circumstances we face into the future.

There are two lessons of life that I want to share with you Lucy.

1. You Are the Equal of Anyone

In many societies, people are treated poorly; they have even been taught and conditioned by the society they live in to think they do not have the standing or rights of others. This is patently not true. I have met many people in all sorts of roles in my working life: Prime Ministers and State Premiers, political, corporate, government agency and community leaders, managers, office and trades workers, and in all honesty, I can say I haven't seen any qualities or capabilities that put one set of leaders, managers or workers above any others in importance or ability. Be confident that you deserve respect from others as much as you should offer yours in whatever situations: work, community or personal, that you may face.

So don't be afraid of finding the purpose in your life that you were brought into this world to seek and pursue. It's wise to beware of those that will seek to exploit you, but don't let that be a barrier to being open to working with others in an honest and constructive way.

2. Everyone Is Your Equal

Every person has the right of their opinion, to have enough to sustain their lives, to education, freedom from abuse and to find a useful place for themselves in this world. By looking everyone in the eye and acknowledging them as your equal, you will see so many barriers to your own growth, ambitions and intentions disappear.

On one hand, you should not allow others to push you down, exploit or abuse you, but on the other you should not allow gender, race, disability, or other societal factors like financial wealth distort your views, treatment or respect of others.

It is harder than we think to do this because we are conditioned by society and our own experiences to generalise and make assumptions, in fact, we build up 'blind spots' to our own poor behaviours. It also takes a lot of courage to recognise and take action to overcome many of our own prejudices, especially if we find they are accepted ways of thinking in the circles in which we move.

Be courageous but humble and do what is right, and you will find that any short term pain that may be experienced is rewarded many times over in the longer term.

> *Why would people put others down, when there is so much to be gained in lifting them up.*

It is *kindness* that is such a big part of your life, Lucy. Not just kindness you share but kindness generously given to you at your times of need and development in growing into a beautiful woman in heart, body, and mind. When we look at what has enabled us to succeed at any stage of life, we can always find someone who has helped us, whether it is parents, friends, teachers or mentors. Your journey as a child has shaped your kind heart, with so much support from those who care. You attend a great school where the qualities of kindness and wellbeing are supported, your mother supports and takes you to netball, dance classes and social events, and you have loving family support from so many people in your life.

As you grow through your teenage years and adulthood, more and more responsibility rests with you, Lucy, in the choices you make. This includes how you translate life's experiences into your own values and beliefs and sustain your bodily, mental and spiritual well-being.

Kindness is a critical part of love and a hallmark of enduring relationships. It is not often recognised, may not be returned for many years, and can require personal sacrifice, but it will always make you better for the giving.

Being the best person we can be gives us countless rewards as we face all that our life's journey reveals, providing a compass to guide us through confusion and hardship as obstacles arise, and building wonderful relationships and treasured moments all along the way.

To sustain a kind and generous heart, you must be kind to yourself too. You must develop the strength to withstand challenges, pain and even unfairness that the world may throw at you. So:

- **Be kind to your body** – look after your health by finding joy in exercise and play, balance in diet, recognising it is a gift given to you as it carries you through a fruitful and happy life.
- **Be kind to your mind** – learn and develop it, understand when it is leading you into negative thinking and emotions, give it opportunity for rest and meditation, and build habits that reflect the best of what you are and can be.
- **Be kind to your heart (spirit)** – discover and value what is the essence of you, that which brings you joy and that which guides you in your choices and beliefs. Look beyond the physical to the spiritual and intentionally pursue joy and purpose in your life.

Strong, generous and kind people take up that challenge. They do not see themselves as just victims of others' actions or life's circumstances, and their beauty shines through. That is my wish for you Lucy, and all the children of today and tomorrow.

We Need the Qualities of Kindness Throughout Our Changing World!

Now is a time of enormous change. The magnitude of this change is such that while it is starting to affect everyone's lives, no-one could hope to understand the depth or breadth of the consequences.

It is through times such as these that our human qualities of kindness, empathy and integrity are critical to determining the quality of life that we shall have in the future.

Some massive changes are underway. One of the major areas of technology development in our time is in artificial intelligence (AI). Scientists and engineers have developed self-learning computers and devices, and some predict there will soon be a time that AI will be so advanced that it will not have the capability to communicate the complexity of its developed understandings to human beings. Where will that leave us!

The use of technology and AI in scientific discovery will unlock truths and opportunities that are going to have enormous benefit to society. We are now seeing huge advances in medical technologies, transport, data management and computation, virtual reality, as just some examples.

This progress is not always about putting humans first though. Computers, robotics and systems are taking over a myriad of repetitious tasks from humans and are also moving to more complex services that were once only the field of highly trained and experienced professionals. Machine and computer self-learning technologies are being heavily invested in as countries and companies strive to gain competitive advantage.

Technology advances have always been with us, but we are at a technical and social tipping point like no other time in human history as computer software systems reach the stage of greater intelligence than people. As the huge drive by companies and governments to implement these for strategic economic and military advantage happens, we shall see these systems having increasing control over the lives of us all.

I take pride in the engineering profession, which is where I began my career, as it operated with a code of ethics. Engineering is guided by ethics as it applies scientific principles to create facilities, equipment and infrastructure to fundamentally serve the requirements of communities: medicine, architecture, law, university-based science and research all operate in a similar manner.

However, a new flavour of technological innovation now has popular focus. It is disruptive of existing systems, commercially driven and most often employs far less people than the industries it displaces. Often, these emerge outside of a professional body held to a code of ethics, and because regulators are so far behind the introduced technologies and associated business models, the new systems do not have the same consumer/customer safeguards or regulation as the traditional ones they are displacing.

AI needs to be programmed to incorporate ethics, and the challenges of how this may develop as societies' social norms and ethical standards continue to evolve and mature are before us.

Could societal decision-making actually be improved, through such systems, to deliver high quality, bias-free learning and application? Internationally, people are becoming disenchanted and distrustful of governments and major corporations, and they may regard objective and data based decision-making systems as an improved option in time. For example, the funding of key human services, such as health and education programs, are constantly changing, with funding being reprioritised based on politics of the day. Systems that continually assess innovation, program success and managed funding distribution, accordingly, would potentially cost less and deliver improved outcomes for the community, over those of political decision-making.

Can intelligent systems be taught ethics in the same manner that they incorporate other learnings, through the massive data-sets that develop AI currently? I believe so, with time, but the key factor now is the initial program development. We can expect that the ethical safeguards within AI systems, if they do exist, will reflect the ethics of the organisations or individuals developing them. If the human qualities we treasure are not a part of the thinking and culture of the corporations developing AI, there is little hope of the systems functioning in an ethical manner. It may even be incapable of learning to do so.

This emphasises the importance of changing the focus, leadership and decision-making of major corporations from one that is built to deliver commercial outcomes for its owners, to one that has a more mature and balanced outlook on global social good and sustainability.

Dear Lucy, isn't this what your parents and teachers have taught? I know you understand that when dealing with people we can't just take from others; they must be treated with respect no matter what their circumstances, and we must look after the place where we live. The laws of our land and in countries across the world gave companies many of the same rights as people (and even over people) centuries ago, but the laws of those times didn't require companies to have a social and environmental conscience, let alone have the responsibilities you and I have, to try to make this a better place to live.

We need to ensure that control of the future and well-being of people is not left by default with major corporations and their advancing technology. We cannot be confident that they have the ethical expectations of society incorporated within their guiding principles, and the world we live in can no longer sustain the drive and appetite for economic expansion that they currently voraciously pursue.

The 'humanisation' of major organisations and corporations with values like kindness, care and empathy, enabled by AI and technologies, is what our future requires; overcoming many of the social, economic and environmental challenges we face. This is not just for the good of the global community, but also for those who work within.

We need to become global citizens, global communities, global nations.

Not abandoning our beliefs, cultures or national pride; but celebrating these and those of other peoples.

Becoming people who give more than they take from this world. Making a net positive contribution to society and environment through the unique skills and abilities that are our individual gifts.

Global people coming together in communities and building globally responsible nations.

3

Dear Flora

Reach out when your heart tells you to reach out.

You are such a joyful child of the universe. Your little smile lights up any room, bringing anyone in your presence out of any worldly worries into a state of happiness for just being there to share that moment with you. As a toddler you're so inquisitive, climbing up on anything you spy, opening cupboards, drawers and boxes, picking up anything on the ground, taking delight in any flower, plant, animal, bird or fish that comes your way.

We must ensure that this pure love of life and the world you live in is not lost or diminished as you appreciate it all so fully that one would be excused for thinking that Creation itself was made for children, people just as you!

How do we put a value on that: all the different plants, animals, and the lands and waters that hold them?

The trade-offs between natural environments and the industrial or agricultural landscapes that are required to feed and host mankind have, after all, been made since early humans walked the Earth. But the pendulum has swung too far now, the balance disrupted and so a new way of achieving a globally sustainable way forward is needed.

> *"Today the ecological crisis has assumed such proportions as to be the responsibility of everyone...*
> *The greenhouse effect has now reached crisis proportions..."*
> *- Pope John Paul II, Peace with All Creation, 1990*

What, I wonder, would government, business and community look like if we adopted your way of looking at our worldly environment, Flora? All the excitement, curiosity and discovery that we could imagine, yet always with an indelible love of and commitment to our natural environment. We certainly wouldn't be sitting still, nor would there be any doubt about acting to address environmental issues... and now!

I could see an enormous unlocking of opportunities for individuals as they engaged in truly responsive, socially and environmentally focussed companies and organisations. Just imagine the enormous social and environmental innovation and transformational change that could be gained from the vast corporate capabilities, skills and minds that are currently in pursuit of economic advantage being unlocked for the benefit of all. The true potential of people would ascend.

> *Linking organisational purpose to global sustainability goals is becoming increasingly recognised as a critical factor for successful enterprises.*

Benefits are being generated in employee attraction, retention and pro-ductivity; customer loyalty; brand value; and cost savings; improving bottom-line outcomes.

Significant business advantage can be achieved in incorporating social and environmental objectives into company missions, values and activities; therefore, it is not suggested that organisations must pay a price. Their global potential can be unleashed too.

The Boston Consulting Group (BCG) points to a growing rift between tech companies that are playing such a big part in shaping the future of society and broader society itself. BCG suggests companies should adopt an expanded Purpose [5]. They urge companies to look beyond the needs of customers and shareholders (as important as these are) to an expanded *Purpose 2.0*, where serving societal needs is also fundamental to the company's direction.

Government could look a lot different too. A lot less politicking on issues critical to community would be expected to start with, but government would also have much greater capacity to be pro-active in the setting of policy and controls. It could have a greater focus on supporting, guiding, and rewarding positive, sustainable behaviours and capacity building. The bigger picture would be outcomes that support global success in terms of commercial, social and environmental capital.

If community and business are striving for social and environmental good, it should lead to less regulatory controls and enforcement, less resources spent in prosecuting poor behaviours and in cleaning up the mess left from thoughtless behaviour.

In the world where people lead us forward with the wonderful qualities of the beautifully spirited little girl who is you Flora, our environment and the people around us would always come first. We would see amazing transformations in work, our quality of life and innovation, while continually looking forward to the next challenge.

United

Many of us across the world believe in the spiritual dimensions of Love, and even in the existence of a God of Love (even if we see or understand God differently), this unites us.

Even more believe in spirituality, and that unites us.

Many believe in the beauty of the world and universe, and that adds to our unity.

Leaving very few, when you think about it.

We have a collective responsibility to the amazing creation that is this world, and to one another, to preserve the quality of love and beauty of our existence.

However, we are failing this task and, in these times so frequently impacted by natural disasters, it's as if the world had been given permission to strike back, given the abuse it has suffered at our collective hands.

Time to value and treat creation kindly if we expect to dwell harmoniously within it.

4

Dear Sunny

May every challenge and demand you face be just another step in your growth, and allow it to be no more than that which adds to the depth and beauty of your character.

In 2019 we welcomed you into our lives, Sunny! A dear little baby boy who featured in our local newspaper within a day or so of being born (you may have to look up what a newspaper is in 2050 I imagine). One of two babies born on Father's Day in our city, you certainly pushed your Dad and Grandad out of the Father's Day spotlight when you decided to come into the world a bit earlier than expected!

A baby so cute, small and fragile, and only just starting to share with us who you are. You grow and develop so quickly, taking in so much of what is around you and adapting to the world outside the womb. It is a highly protective and loving environment you live in now; with the care and sustenance you require provided by your loving Mum and Dad.

Already I can see a resilience growing though, a strength supported by those bonds, something that will stand you in good stead for the challenges of living in a significantly different world to that I was born into some 65 years before.

I suspect you are going to continue to express your presence just as you did on Father's Day 2019, stepping forward when circumstances call. The strong family, community and sustainability ethic of the family you are growing up in, makes that a very good thing.

Too often the voice of good people is drowned by propaganda and distorted information emanating from politics or self-interest. In a computer age, we should be moving to a future where reliable data, facts and information is much easier for all to access, yet the virtually incomprehensible computing power and massive connecting networks of social media are far too often the tools of misinformation and persuasion rather than to listen to and respond to community.

We need strong, resilient, and wise people with a global sustainability ethic to see manipulation for what it is. We need them to help harness technology and innovation to improve the way we do things and to inform decisions with accurate, truthful information and research data.

And we need principled men and women who have empathy for those who face disadvantage or who may be in a tough spot when they happen to encounter them.

The reason why is simple. The world we live in now sees many people, both close to us and far removed, being subject to enormous injustices and catastrophic events that seem grossly unfair. When encountering these, the qualities that strong, empathetic, and principled young men like you are growing to be, Sunny, can bring hope to the situation. The little boy who loves to play Spiderman now can be one of the real-life superheroes that the world needs more of to become a fairer and safer place for the vulnerable in our society.

Empathy and understanding are fundamental to the right approach. It's hard when faced with destructive, self-serving behaviours to not let anger direct our response to the arrogance or violence, but this just takes us down the same path of behaviour that we initially thought so bad.

Understanding is the key to finding the pathway that will lift you up and enable you to look beyond bad behaviours and dire circumstances, and to respond compassionately in a manner that takes you to the right outcomes.

Treating others with respect, and as a man especially, treating women with respect, is such an important part of an individual's evolving growth. Sunny, you will have your part to play in making the world more equitable, just, and fundamentally happy; whether it be in family, the community you live in or in broader society. Embrace the challenge and be brave enough to stand up and be counted even when distorted social norms suggest you do otherwise.

I can see wonderful qualities in you at the age of 4, Sunny, that will make you a great *defender* of vulnerable people. You have a wonderful example in your Mum, who is working for an organisation that is assisting women who have faced harm in their lives. There is much you can learn from your parents about being a compassionate defender.

We need wisdom to make the right choices and responses. Violence is rarely the right choice but in exceptional circumstances may be the only one. The people of Ukraine did not have an option but to take up arms and fight, when Russia's government leaders decided to invade their country, and the cost to millions of innocent people has been terrible, on both sides.

Compassion is an essential quality of people in government to ensure truly effective and socially responsive systems are in place, supported by mechanisms to prevent those with self-serving agendas finding ways to manipulate people, voters or systems to serve their own ends.

If we can harness the best of learnings, acknowledge mistakes, and seek the best outcomes for society, new (or renewed) democratic models may emerge. These will lead to better government decision-making and processes, leveraging technology to support policy setting. However, these models, the technological systems and democratic principles that they are founded upon must have high integrity. They need to be rigorously monitored and protected so they do not become instruments to divide and manipulate for political advantage or self-interest.

And as society moves toward an uncertain future, the voices of our children need to be heard, now more urgently than ever before.

5

Hear Our Call... Through Time & Space

Listen to our Voice; we are your Children's Children,
As each day passes, hope diminishes.
"Puzzled as we are as to why you delay".

A hand reaches to yours like a newborn's clasp;
Awakened now to the presence that has bridged the gap
– time no longer the barrier to realisation of consequence.

It is more than blood;
It is more than bone,
That the passage of time and generations will hone,
In the bond that binds you, me and them,
As we face the legacy we have passed on.

You open your eyes to your Children's children;
They look into yours with love and trust,
Secure in the parental bond that protects and nurtures.
Feel their heartbeat as they move closer to your breast,
Seeking warmth and reassurance of inter-generational parentage.

Open your ears to the sounds of their breath,
Labouring to squeeze life-giving oxygen from air,
That carries the residuals of your existence and industry.
"Father, Mother, Nanna, Papa" they call you, by child given name,
Knowing the essence within is the same.

It is more than blood;
It is more than bone,
That the passage of time and generations will hone,
In the bond that binds you, me and them,
As we face the legacy we have passed on.

Each time we take from earth, air or community of now,
Beyond which it can sustain and renew,
We take a hundred, a thousand times that sum,
From that of their time on this world to come.

Before the age of impact and destruction,
There's time to make change with little consequence today.
"Puzzled as we are as to why you delay".

Which shall it be? The choice is yours and ours to make.
Listen to the Voice of our Children's children... for all our sakes!

And now, as anguish grows, the trembling is unstoppable.

The heaving breath slowly fades to silence and desolation prevails.

The hand goes limp and you disengage.

The bridge that briefly existed crumbles and fades.

You don't hear the cries and will never know if they still call to the ones that

chose today's excess before their tomorrow.

But the Eden that once was still circles in space,

Quieter now, set free, of the pace and the course set by humanity.

"Puzzled as we are to why you delay"

There is a better choice, a better way.

But wait — see the trembling abate,

And the glimmer that awakes in those trusting eyes,

The gentle breath and warmth that flows in the comfort that trust has grown,

From confidence that you now understand.

And as the generations come, grow and move through, the circle of life that is a

gift from you, always their right as it was yours,

Beauty in place and in spirit becomes what it was pre-determined to be:

- in peace and harmony

It is more than blood;

It is more than bone,

That the passage of time and generations will hone,

In the bond that binds you, me and them,

As we face the legacy we have passed on.

6

Renaissance 2.0 — Riches Beyond Wealth

Remember that many must drink from the well, and if you take more than the Earth can provide or others can spare, it is you too who will find it dry.

When we think about what we want for our children's future, there are the tangibles, such as physical health, food, clothing, education, success in their careers and a safe and beautiful physical environment, and the intangibles, like appreciation, love, joy and spiritual wellbeing. Inspired by this, we should seek this in the communities we live in, across our nation and for the good of humankind across the globe. We should strive for a healthy and sustainable planet Earth.

The *Renaissance* (French for rebirth) was a period of European history that emerged from the dark and feudal times of the Middle Ages. It was a time where magnificent artworks, architectural structures and cities emerged that are recognised today as some of the most outstanding and beautiful creations of humanity. This came from deliberate efforts to move society forward with renewed thinking, recognising the beauty of humanity and nature. People sought to celebrate that through the arts, building cities that were for all, and pursuing the most noble qualities.

It was a period of innovation and invention, one that incorporated creativity and arts, leaving us with an extraordinary legacy today. The magnificent cities of Florence, Venice and Rome; the priceless artworks of Da Vinci's Mona Lisa, Raphael's School of Athens fresco, and Michelangelo's Sistine Chapel ceiling fresco and statue of David are just some obvious examples.

The Renaissance period revealed how leadership, creativity and appreciation of the beauty of creation can lead society to enjoy healthy growth and communal well-being, even out of the dark periods of our history.

The School of Life provides an insight on how taking a new look at the way we view the world, in particular seeking the common good, has produced extraordinary social and economic advances in past ages. This same paradigm could serve humanity extraordinarily well into the future [6].

Our schools and training institutions are focussed on Science, Technology, Engineering and Mathematics, (STEM) subjects and disciplines, to prepare people for anticipated jobs of the future, but something is missing. A strong movement is pursuing adding the Arts as a further major factor (making STEAM). This is consistent with what helped the people of the Renaissance period in their innovation, creativity, and quality of design for the good of the communities of those times.

Further lessons of the Renaissance are the harnessing of *Purposeful Passion** for the good of society and incorporating perspective in design and works. The arts are a prime vehicle in achieving a rebirth of social and economic thinking that align with these important characteristics.

*More in Chapter 8, on Power of Purposeful Passion

From Industry 4.0 to Renaissance 2.0

We have entered a period regarded as the Fourth Industrial Revolution, where technology is delivering substantial industrial change. An industrial ethos prevails, continuing the path that puts industrial growth before other parameters. Industry 4.0 will soon morph to Industry 5.0, 6.0 and on it will go, with relegation of social well-being and quality of environment to secondary considerations.

The Australian Government is excited by the potential of Industry 4.0 because it sees the new wave of technological advances substantially offsetting traditional challenges of high labour costs and distance to markets, providing a major boost to Australia's economic competitiveness. However, as everything is in some way connected, cutting labour costs has employment and social implications that must be recognised and responsibly managed. The time of siloing innovation and advancing economic outcomes in the singular pursuit of competitive advantage needs to be drawn to an end.

We need to create a new context in which we move beyond seeing future economic success in terms of greater financial and operational efficiency, primarily created through technological advances. If we wish a more socially just and environmentally sustainable world, we need government, industry and commerce to integrate these elements into the very core of our next stage of societal and industrial development.

How can we move our society from an Industry 4.0 mindset to a second Renaissance?

Balancing the Books

In virtually every way, monetary capital and cashflows govern our personal lives, the organisations we may work in, government systems and services, and affect the strength and resilience of nations. Governments and corporations develop financial budgets to fund all the services and works they plan to undertake, and they use established accounting practices to manage and control their finances.

When it comes to social and environmental considerations though, they are managed separately, in numerous different ways. Ultimately, they are controlled by a myriad of laws, regulations and adjustments, based on community expectations and the organisation's own application of social, national and organisational values.

The Renaissance was led by wealthy patrons who began the journey by firstly looking back at historic success and wisdom and then building on that with the contemporary perspective of their time. Taking from their example, we should not necessarily abandon existing systems, rather, look at what has worked well with a new perspective (a lunar outlook) and develop our new way forward from that starting point.

We spend our working life earning money to pay for living costs and if we can save a bit after that to accumulate some wealth, in the form of a house, car, or investment assets we are fortunate.

Companies sell services and goods and if they cover their costs they make profits, which they can pay as dividends to the owners, accumulate to fund future growth or invest in assets.

Fundamentally, after meeting ongoing costs, companies and us as individuals want to build financial wealth. In business practice this is represented by the Accounting Equation. In essence it is simply stating that the wealth we have consists of *what we own, less what we owe.*

As simple as this equation is, when you reflect on it there is probably nothing that you or I could contemplate that has had such a powerful impact on the entirety of modern mankind. And in this age, there is probably nothing that exists that could not have a theoretical monetary value assigned to it.

Business, government and our own financial aspirations are summed up by this equation.

In the financial terms of business:

> *The Equity of an entity is equal to the Assets it holds less its Liabilities.*

The all-prevailing application of this equation drives organisations, governments, gets people out of bed, feeds, clothes and provides for our lifestyles – or doesn't (if we don't have the capital).

For an everyday household such as my own (chasing the Australian dream of home ownership), it could translate to:

> *Our financial wealth (equity) is equal to the value of our house, car, our super fund and bank balances, and any further assets we have, less the house mortgage, personal loans and unpaid bills.*

In broad terms, pursuit of wealth as defined by this simple equation has served us well. It has been a useful paradigm around which we have built the rules of commerce and many of the laws that govern our everyday lives, which, overall, has seen a raising of global living standards (with some dramatic exceptions of course).

But it is now failing.

What we learnt in science class, the principle of action and reaction, cause and effect, also applies to the world we live in and are taking from. It affects all of society. With the expansion of global financial wealth in the past decades – and its concentration at the top end of town – it did not encapsulate important facets of social good and environmental stewardship. In fact, the reliance on fossil fuels for industrial growth has been a primary cause of environmentally damaging greenhouse gas emissions. The widening gap between rich and poor across communities and nations has led to social inequity and disharmony. The impact of corporate pursuit of financial maximisation and destructive human activities on the environment is evident in the increased ferocity and frequency of floods and fires, heatwaves, extinction of animal and plant species and decline in polar ice caps.

The good (or even the survival) of humankind, including governments and major corporates, is no longer effectively served by an equation/ paradigm that does not factor in environmental benefit or disbenefit, nor social benefit or impact. Our Earthly environment is finite and can no longer give without return; similarly, our global community needs to be treated equitably and will not withstand an ongoing process of net loss of many to accommodate the net financial gain by a fewer number of privileged entities.

Enterprise-Driven Kindness and Care

Every company needs to create benefits from its activities, but this doesn't need to be confined to financial ones. It can be for social good or an outcome for our natural world.

Can we imagine a world in which corporate enterprises were a major contributor to social good and environmental restoration?... *Enterprise Driven Kindness* and *Care for Nature,* an intrinsic part of the way corporate enterprise worked, and a fundamental paradigm of our society! Taking the very mechanisms that have been the success of economic growth and then harnessing them for the benefit of people, the Earth and nature. What we can conceive and achieve if we embrace new thinking could be extraordinary. Our future outlook need not be overshadowed by climate driven extremes, social decline and poverty, but instead one dominated by improved living standards, sustainable prosperity and restoration of natural beauty.

If we want social equity, then it needs to be built into our major activities! Why would it even be allowable for an organisation or nation to build wealth at the disadvantage of others and not account for that cost?

If we want a sustainable environment, then we must apply accountability and cost to any entity that takes from it. How can it be reasonable to do otherwise in a world now under threat of massive environmental decline and consequential human cost?

It goes beyond the *user pays* concept though, it is about harnessing the passion of people through them buying into a new vision for our world and its future that is on offer through *Renaissance 2.0.* Latent passion that sits dormant within corporations, governments and us as individuals living day to day, its potential unrealised due to a lack of unifying leadership and vision.

Where to start?

Global Equity: Wealth Redefined

We actually have a solid starting point for a new way forward hidden in the proven methodologies of accounting equations, practices and adopted financial standards; we just need to modify these in a way that financial benefit is balanced with social and environmental equity. To enable the change so urgently necessary, the ethos of balanced *Global Equity* needs to be incorporated into our thinking and how we account for our actions.

> *"We cannot solve our problems with the same thinking we used when we created them." - Albert Einstein*

Perhaps the rules of finance and economics are not part of our conscious everyday thinking, but they quietly sit there as part of our psyche and have a significant role in determining how we act and plan our lives. Building an equally powerful mechanism which incorporates the further complementary dimensions of social equity and environmental equity becomes a tool to assist in driving the actions of people, corporations, communities and governments. The aim: to achieve a socially just and environmentally sustainable future for society.

What would this mean in practical terms? It would see all organisations, businesses and governments adopting new accounting practices based on holistic approaches where their Global Equity is determined. Not just financial equity, as currently determined through the Accounting

Equation but also Social Equity and Environmental Equity. Specifically, determining and reporting what benefit they have created through their operations towards improving society and the environment.

Global Equity then becomes the overarching driver of the organisation's objectives, incorporating Financial Equity as it has traditionally been known, but only after it has been balanced with Social Equity and Environmental Equity outcomes.

The good news is, the journey has already begun on so many fronts and we have solid foundations to build on to establish a sustainable future. An evolution is underway. In many cases, subtle changes are occurring that will generate substantial positive global outcomes; recycling, waste minimisation, water and energy conservation are becoming the normal way of life for many. Renewable energy development and use, electrification of plant and vehicles, and life cycle planning in product development are just some of the signs we see of maturing business and government practices.

What would the all-powerful Accounting Equation that has brought us to where we sit today look like when we factor in the social and environmental parameters?

Building the New Accounting Tool

In order to create a Global Equity Equation, Social Equity and Environmental Equity need to be determined and quantified.

No small task, as this has to be in the same terms if it is to make sense. Namely, they would all be measured in monetary values. We can't apply equal consideration and accountability to financial benefits, social benefits or environmental benefits unless they are all valued in a common way. And, what has not been calculated into dollars in this age? Insurance companies put a value on arms, legs, trauma and physical assets; governments build financial budgets on health, education, community services against defined needs and environmental remediation works, and carbon credits have market values.

Social Equity will be positive as a result of activities, where benefits to society exceed negative impacts upon it.

Conversely, social equity is reduced if negative social impacts exceed benefits. Building social value is a prime function of government, but many of their activities require a balance to be struck. For example, they are often faced with situations where they may have to take land and demolish existing infrastructure, such as housing, in order to build and provide other social infrastructure, such as schools or hospitals. Methods already exist to quantify the social impact and value of these activities in monetary terms.

Similarly, Environmental Equity is increased where positive environmental outcomes from an organisation's activities exceed negative impacts. Mining companies undertake rehabilitation works with the goal of re-establishing the natural vegetation and animal species after their mining works, but often undertake further efforts such as revegetating other cleared land or contributing to environmental research to provide further positive environmental outcomes.

And Environmental Equity is reduced when we fail to adequately address environmental factors. The huge number of discarded and unrehabilitated mine pits across the Australian landscape are prime examples.

Both Social Equity and Environmental Equity need to be quantified into the same objective monetary terms as Financial Equity in order to incorporate them into a single *Equation for Global Equity*.

The Equation for Global Equity then serves to facilitate understanding of the interactions between an organisation's operations and the social and natural environment in which it exists. It can become a driver of environmental and social entrepreneurship and development, and mechanism of accountability, regulation and responsible governing: working in a similar way to the Accounting Equation's effect on industrial growth and in building financial wealth. The concept of Global Equity can apply to us as individuals, families, regions, companies, organisations or countries, in the same manner that Financial Equity can apply to any entity.

> *Global Equity * is equal to the Financial Equity, plus the Social Equity and the Environmental Equity of an entity.*

> ** See Appendix for more on the Global Equity Equation*

The Roadmap

There is a lot to be done to put the concept of a Global Equity Equation into practical use for organisations, business corporations and government. At some future point it may be used by individuals too, but focussing on the larger entities first has the greatest potential for early benefit.

The Renaissance period extended over three centuries. What our world needs is urgent attention to critical environmental issues and social impacts affecting millions, while developing new ways forward that build a positive sustainable future and take us away from repeating cycles of social and environmental decay.

The Global Equity concept is not a quick fix. Unfortunately, if it is not properly developed, trialled, and evaluated, it may have greater social harm than good. It is a journey!

Looking for early wins with corporate and government support may generate critical change and momentum to carry the process forward.

Basic steps envisaged include:

- Defining Environmental Equity, Environmental Benefit and Environmental Detriment, and Social Equity, Social Benefit and Social Detriment in a way that each can be applied to the Global Equity Equation.
- Determine standards for the environmental and social parameters that are complementary to those of established accounting standards.
- Develop priorities for implementation that address pressing social and environmental issues but are realistic in implementation.
- Determine methods and develop monetary values for social and environmental outcomes for application.
- Establish incentive programs, revised regulations and an expanded taxation framework to support the new Global Equity accounting system.
- Review, learn and improve.

As logical as accounting for environment and social factors may be, the massive task of doing so is not underestimated. However, what may have been an impossible task a decade ago is far more achievable now because of the extensive work done in environmental assessments and in quantifying social value. Additionally, we now have enormous data processing and computing power to crunch the data and process the algorithms necessary to make the necessary dollar value determinations.

There has been substantial international work done in establishing sustainability goals [7], and to quantify Social Value [8] and to value Natural Resources in monetary terms.

Natural Capital Accounting [9] is being increasingly utilised to put value on naturally existing environment assets and to quantify their utilisation at local, regional and national levels.

Having worked with many businesses and industries over my career, I am aware that many would cringe at the perceived administrative burden of applying the balanced global equation and supporting accounting systems to their operations. Meanwhile, others would welcome the recognition and benefits a transparent system would bring to the significant efforts they are already putting into benefiting the communities and environment(s) in which they currently operate. It would also serve to 'level the playing field' between companies that do the right thing by society and the environment, in helping them compete against those who ignore detrimental impacts.

Development and adoption of such a comprehensive accounting system needs to be a well-managed, transitionary process; voluntary, at least initially, with significant government, professional and scientific input to streamline processes, to determine values and costs across the social and environmental parameters, and to develop and transition into new regulatory frameworks and taxation systems. New tax systems and regulatory requirements should be equitably applied to those who operate at a cost to the broader community and our environment but should also support the efforts of those that mitigate adverse impacts or indeed provide benefits. Government must also look at incentives and how it can remove barriers, allowing socially and environmentally responsible entities to thrive.

The major benefits include a more complete set of levers to work with in planning and shaping future direction beyond those currently available, and result in unleashing talent and potential to drive sustainable and socially responsible growth.

It would require new thinking, leadership and governance practice and a shift away from the profit-driven ones held today. This traditional thinking is well entrenched, as I found in early 2019 when I undertook a Board Directors course at a respected institution that delivers highly regarded, contemporary training to company directors across Australia and internationally. One of the most fundamental duties of a Board Director is their duty to the organisation/company, known as fiduciary duty. At this course, participants were asked the question, *to whom does a Director owe a Duty, is it to society?* After spending virtually my whole career in organisations providing services to community, I immediately jumped in with 'Of course they do!' and of course I was incorrect. The most basic duty a director holds is to the company/organisation they serve. The law of the day required this and any Director that put societal or environmental considerations before company interests may have done so at personal financial and legal risk.

I can only imagine how absurd this would sound to people, our children, of 2050, when today thousands of scientists across the world have warned loud and clear of the impacts on the Earth of global warming. The consequences of those catastrophic impacts predicted would be all around you (with global temperature rise of 1.5 to 4 degrees) by 2050. This is why fundamental drivers such as the all-prevailing Accounting

Equation needs to be changed to include social and environmental factors, so they too become fundamental to our way of acting and doing business now and into the future.

Financial reports are front and centre in all organisations and government agencies, often reviewed weekly by CEOs and senior managers, and even shareholders typically have access to quarterly financials and detailed reports at their Annual Meetings. The same level of attention is necessary for the social and environmental elements of an entity's operations and forward plans if a sustainable balance is to be achieved.

Imagine how our lives and world would flourish if as much attention was paid to this every day and every week, as we do in trying to build economic outcomes. If we put the same effort into making our own and others' lives better, and had time and incentive to put work into improving the environment we live in.

These principles can be applied to our personal lives, as a family, at a community level, to companies, organisations of every kind, government, country, or the planet.

Personal Change

As I enter my twilight years, I have a sense of being in a situation in my life that is the sum of all the choices and circumstances of my life's journey. My health is principally the result of what I have eaten, drunk, the decisions to exercise or not. The place I live in is the sum of what I have put into building, maintaining and cultivating our home and property. The community I experience is from the choices to participate and contribute socially. My state of mind and spiritual well-being are an outcome of the choices of good over bad, what I engage in, the practice of my beliefs, values and faith, preparedness to call out or walk away from what I see as destructive, and discipline or mindfulness in keeping true to my values. Like these personal choices, a global equation of what we personally can do in creating personal financial wealth, health of body and mind, nett contribution to community and environment, and to grow in spirituality could also be a useful concept for us to use in building value and quality in our lives.

If we wish to preserve our personal and community well-being, we each must do what is right by the environment and within the community in which we live. While we all live in different circumstances, we can each consciously seek to reduce our footprint on the Earth and be a contributor to community.

The power of personal advocacy should not be underestimated. We are the customers of the major corporates and electors of governments. As the volume and persistence of our collective voices grow, they are compelled to act with greater urgency.

I feel I am one of the richest people on the Earth, not because of any money in the bank but because I have had a wonderful life, have lived in some of the most beautiful coastal communities in Western Australia and in having a family, including my grandchildren Lucy, Flora, Sunny and Rose and all my wonderful children, to enjoy that life with. We all need enough money to live but the greatest wealth is not economic. It is the quality created in living a fulfilling life regardless of the challenges and circumstances faced in that journey, and the value we place on and contribute to the environment in which we live.

Personal wealth redefined!

Organisations & Change

Organisations can drive transformational change and unleash the enormous talent that lies within their people and capabilities by adopting globally sustainable practices and accountability. Already, so many companies are adopting sustainability reporting, and many are choosing to adopt socially and/or environmentally beneficial practices and programs that most often are realising benefits to their financial bottom line as well. A great step forward, but the financial paradigm still rules, and we need to make the further shift to placing equal value on all key pillars of sustainability.

Like John Lennon, I may just be a dreamer, but after 40 plus years in business, community, and government working environments, I can *imagine* a world that I want for my grandchildren, and all children of the future. A positive future achieved by new and re-balanced thinking by us as individuals, businesses, community and governments.

Imagine companies striving every day to improve environmental outcomes from their operations with the same effort put into building profits. Imagine them scouring for opportunities to value-add their offerings with discernible improvements to the lives of the most disadvantaged in our communities. Imagine conservation agencies finding their efforts in restoring threatened species or degraded environments matched with enthused business and community support. Jointly funded and resourced research and technology initiatives developed and directed at the most pressing issues facing our communities.

There are many examples of companies shifting their practices and reaping the benefits. One that I have experienced personally is the development of a Community Branch of the Bendigo Bank in the city where I live. The model is based on a 50:50 profit share, where the Bendigo (*mother*) bank makes profits, community members who invested to establish the local bank are rewarded with competitive dividends, and the community itself has seen the level of the bank's donations to local causes grow from thousands of dollars in the early stages to tens of thousands, and now hundreds of thousands of dollars going to fantastic local projects. The relationship with its customers and the local communities where it operates has established Bendigo Bank as one of the most strongly trusted brands in Australia.

Funds flowing from organisations like the Bendigo Community Banks to local groups and projects build measurable social value and/or environmental outcomes, increasing Global Equity.

Organisational wealth redefined!

Governments & Change

If governments adopted the Global Balanced Equity approach, taxable entities could still maintain free choices of where they direct their resources and efforts, but social and/or environmental detriment would come at a cost to them. By the same token, those demonstrating social or environmental benefit through their accounts would, or perhaps should, be rewarded through the taxation system.

A real challenge to *Enterprise Driven Kindness and Care of Nature* would be for governments to step back and let supply and demand shape the efforts of people and organisations towards the areas of greatest need. Politicians and government bureaucracies love to control (successful) programs and put resources towards priorities that they feel will deliver favourable political outcomes. After all, that is what gets politicians re-elected and department budgets approved.

Certainly, there are major benefits to be had in governments embracing the philosophy of *Renaissance 2.0* and adopting the Global Equation, particularly for their own program and budget development. An area of potential failure arises though if government seeks such a level of control over companies (and citizens) that it is effectively setting the social and environmental priorities for all. Too often, Government efforts in addressing areas of social disadvantage have been dismal failures, and there are many examples of repression and abuse of people in countries that choose to try to control their communities' social beliefs and priorities. Critical to the whole philosophy of *Renaissance 2.0* presented is that it would be enabled by empowered community and corporate leadership, acting with shared vision and passion. It is market driven, not government decreed!

The key then is appropriate governing principles, practices and controls established in advance of implementation, and careful steps forward that are reviewed and improved, based on democratic, inclusive, supportive community values.

It is not government control but incentivising private and public entities to leverage a more holistic and shared commitment to tackling the major challenges before us. It potentially unleashes whole new approaches to the ways we think and act and brings a range of highly competent yet underutilised resources to bear, putting the concept of *Renaissance 2.0* into practice.

How could new thinking and approaches work to engage private enterprise in addressing social inequity? In Australia we currently face a major housing shortage, and with that, a sharp increase in homelessness. Politicians are throwing around proposals such as freezing rents, which has political appeal, despite broad industry advice that this will escalate the problem. This is because private investors, who provide most of the available rental properties, will then cut back in housing investment. An approach based on rewarding those who help solve the problem could come up with a much broader range of potential solutions, ideas such as government tax breaks for holiday home-owners or hotels who provide transitional accommodation to those in need.

Legislative controls are most often developed to prevent the most irresponsible parties from doing what is obviously wrong, but then whole industries get tied up in government 'red tape' as an outcome. Even the most beneficial of projects proposed by companies, ones who are nationally recognised for their high standards of environmental practices, can be held up for years in environmental project approvals.

What if government adopted a tiered system where all companies – due to demonstrated and consistent environmental stewardship – could work their way up a tiered reward hierarchy? They could receive the time and cost benefits of streamlined and facilitated approvals on the basis of solid track records.

A company itself is the best party to understand and address its own environmental or social impacts or opportunities with the greatest efficiency, and most often with greatest effectiveness. They can design products and processes from the outset to deliver greatest benefit, with their deep understanding of the entire processes.

Government has an important role in facilitating this outcome, assisting research effort in a manner that does not leave small and regional businesses behind, setting standards, and setting up a regulatory environment that supports achieving society's desired outcomes.

I am not suggesting I have all the answers. Solutions and frameworks need to be developed with an eye to a sustainable future, in collaboration with industry and community. What I am suggesting is let's seek to bring a broader range of expertise, community ownership and a new set of tools to bear on our critical issues. Ideally, solutions that are supported and owned at the local or regional community level rather than just restricted approaches imposed by government.

Change in government priorities is usually generated from changes we are prepared to make in our own lives. When we look at the volume of plastics, glass, paper and metals discarded around our streets, in rivers, on beaches, parks and roadsides, we get an understanding of just how big the challenge will be in getting people's everyday behaviours to adjust to achieve the positive change a healthy environment requires. I am not saying everyone is littering but the evidence speaks for itself and if each of us thinks about how we can contribute to a better, cleaner world, even the most committed will be able to find ways to do more, perhaps in just sharing their knowledge with others.

It must be initiated by people like you and I, in our own lives and in what we demand of governments and consume as customers. If we act in accord and expect better social and environmental outcomes and accountability, then companies will respond, as will governments as the leaders become inspired... or at least when they realise the political realities of the tidal flow.

AI and the massive data sets which have accumulated can become invaluable tools to enable society's efforts. They can serve to accurately identify and quantify social needs or environmental priorities and assist in matching these with willing corporate and community resources. Computer programs can also be effectively used in achieving rational decision-making processes, development and managing of programs and even predicting outcomes if differing ways forward are contemplated. Reliable and comprehensive data is critical, enabling sound modelling and generating more successful and comprehensive solutions.

Despite these opportunities for social good, the rapid rise of AI for commercial (or military) advantage is raising ethical concerns across communities and within responsible corporations. As well, governments are struggling with the challenges of how to control this on one hand but not lose out on economic advantages AI may offer a nation on the other. The adoption of the principles of a balanced Global Equation and supporting market-driven social good flips the whole issue on its head. If it doesn't serve humanity, it does not grow or prosper.

With a mature and balanced approach to our way of life, facilitated by responsible technology development, substantial progress can be made in addressing social inequities. Positive new opportunities and solutions beyond current imaginations may be our reward. We can move away from a future dominated by fear of impending environmental devastation and human displacement to a period where industrial, social and environmental *renaissance* can be ours, and for our children, to grow and flourish within.

Our national goals and wealth redefined in *Renaissance 2.0.*

> *If wealth is an abundance of valuable things in your life, financial assets will only ever be the smallest part.*

7

Crime Pays

It is the innocent within society who pay the greatest price of crime. Is it time for an 'Abusers Pay' System?

Is it time to revisit the effectiveness of our justice system and related government activities in deterring criminal and anti-social behaviour, and if so, can new tools be brought to bear on these issues to community benefit?

At local and national levels, courtroom tactics have successfully seen court cases abandoned because the alleged victims have been intimidated to such a level that their personal safety or mental health is at threat. This is happening within the very courtrooms and police processes meant to deliver justice or to resolve legal arguments in the parties' and community's best interests. Regardless of guilt or otherwise, the accused parties then walk away. In the case of situations like family court disputes, the bullying and intimidating behaviours can then continue unabated.

Within neighbourhoods across Australian communities, drug houses exist, feeding habits that are fuelling crime, domestic violence, child neglect and destroying the very capabilities of people to lead meaningful lives. These houses may be obvious in the frequent surreptitious visitation of customers day and night, or less so when the operators move to more sophisticated forms of sales and delivery. Often the people involved are available any time of the day, not being tied up by commitments of work,. It is also not uncommon for these illicit business activities to be delivered from government supplied social housing.

Is it conceivable then that not only are current policing and judicial processes failing innocent parties, but also that further government practices are supporting and incubating criminal activities. For example, take a hypothetical situation where people are not working and decided that they wanted to make a living by selling drugs. Chances are, they are on unemployment benefits, are either in social housing or eligible for financial support, have a Commonwealth Government health card providing access to a range of subsidies for their needs: from pharmaceuticals, medical costs to electricity and water charges. Effectively, a basic level of income and support that underpins their situation while they get their illicit business up and running. Of course, it doesn't stop there. The illicit income is untaxed and unreported and so the government support continues, regardless of their business success.

In the previous chapter, the focus was on legitimate business being incentivised and/or taxed based upon how they benefit or detrimentally impact society or the environment, through application of the principle of Global Equity. It begs the question of whether the same approach could be applied to illegal and criminal activities.

In Australia, any business or individual can be subject to a tax audit at the discretion of the Australian Taxation Office (ATO). In fact, it is common business practice to insure against such audits as they can take significant company resources to respond to, with the obligations to demonstrate the business has correctly accounted for all their finances and met their tax obligations. The audited parties are not charged or accused of wrongdoing in advance on the basis of evidence the ATO must justify and prove. Rather the obligation to demonstrate proper practice sits with the company.

If reasonable suspicion exists within the police that illegal activities are being performed to profit from members of society, why then would government not look at investigating the income, assets and capital of the individuals involved and compel them to account for their situation in the same manner the ATO investigates and applies appropriate penalties to tax-paying companies, businesses and individuals?

Further, if ATO, Centrelink and State housing and other relevant agencies collaborated with police and justice agencies with the aim of removing the financial and services support (and tax-free income) that government inadvertently provides to criminal activities and incubation, it may serve as a significant deterrent. No longer would drug dealing or theft be sources of easy cash but instead carry significant financial risk.

Application of the concept of Global Equity to crime may well go beyond looking at taxing profit or inhibiting financial benefit of crime, it may also serve to help redress harm. The approach proposed in adopting Global Equity includes quantifying and putting a monetary value on social and environmental harm, and this could equally be applied to criminal related harm.

The justice system focusses on the alleged perpetrators, in what is an appropriate penalty, but even more so on their rehabilitation, and I'm not suggesting this should not be the case. However, the system largely leaves the victims to find their own means of repairing the damage and coping with their personal suffering. The reality is that very few people have the means to do so. They may carry the consequences for years – or even their lifetime.

If the perpetrator is a large organisation, the victim risks all they have in seeking compensation through the courts.

If it is a domestic violence or sexual assault case, they risk their reputation, mental health and in some situations, the safety of themselves and their children, if they challenge the perpetrators or seek compensation for the inflicted harm.

The proposition that criminal activities are financially penalised is not just aimed at boosting government resources to address crime and impacts on the broad community, or to act as a further deterrent, it is also proposed to be a means of providing real and tangible support to the victims. Victims are largely ignored as they try to re-establish their lives and cope with the callous processes that may prevail in current systems.

Collaboration between agencies would be a critical success factor, however, great care would be needed in design and development of such as system as it could be a huge and unfair burden on innocent people if incorrectly applied. It would also place significant powers into the hands of bureaucrats and accordingly would require independent oversight and processes of appeal.

The principle of *Abuser Pays* is likely to appeal to many but its success would be in the implementation. This needs to be careful, thoughtful, fair and incremental.

There can be no argument that victims of crime, who are usually the most vulnerable in our society, deserve much greater support than what they receive. The major issue is: where do the funds to provide this come from? Adopting the logic of Global Equity suggests they come from the perpetrators!

8

Power of Purposeful Passion

The arts were pivotal in the success of the Renaissance; they were at the core of the city development, architecture, and iconic artworks that we celebrate today, and are no less important to our futures. The arts unleash creativity and passion; capture beauty, qualities and vulnerabilities in people, landscapes and objects; tell stories and convey messages in a manner that many of us would struggle to communicate in words. Most of all, they lead us to an appreciation of circumstances outside our own and can inspire and open us to differing perspectives.

Application of the arts need not be siloed in buildings, monuments and galleries; this outlook can be taken into the boardrooms too. I have used art in facilitating the development of Mission Statements, Purpose and Values for organisational clients as exercises to engage all participants and to stimulate creative thinking. This has generated inspiring free-flowing artworks representing people, inter-linking themes and networks, and images of love, beauty and common purpose. Who would not want to be part of organisations like that!

Not-for-profit organisations are typically filled with people passionate to achieve the vision and purpose because they know they are working for the fundamental good of community. So, it makes sense that expanding the mission of corporations with social and/or environmental objectives opens up a far wider range of opportunities for the passionate engagement of employees and customer buy-in.

Passion and commitment require *faith* in the organisation, where team members put their trust in how it undertakes its business, and where they see an alignment of their personal values and aspirations with that of the organisation.

The organisation's challenge is achieving a holistic mission that incorporates social, environmental and financial objectives that are mutually complementary and viable. These objectives must be sensibly aligned to its capabilities and aspirations, and to those of its people. Success comes from doing what we can do well; maintaining faith, passion and belief in what the organisation is about and what it delivers.

Among the many potential benefits to organisations adopting broader and balanced objectives, perhaps the most significant would be the empowerment and growth of their people. People would be engaged for their *passion* and the organisation becomes a vehicle for their personal and professional growth, skills and knowledge development. Benefits would include their loyalty and commitment. This level of commitment is lacking in many organisations today, despite society's expectation of high levels of ethical and social responsibility to be displayed in modern working environments.

A change in prevailing organisational mindset is proposed...

From: Seeking to align diverse personal values and thinking of employees to that of the organisation's Mission, Purpose and Values;

To: Creation or transformation of organisations to clusters of people with shared Passion and objectives.

We are at a point in history which has opened up the opportunity for change towards more sustainable living and greater social equity across our communities. It is not just the compounding impacts of climatic change driving the re-think but other significant global events also. The Coronavirus (Covid-19) pandemic, in particular, forced changes and resulted in people across the world taking a whole new look at what is important to them in their lives, their future. In many cases, they made wholesale changes in how they work, live and conduct business.

Communities have also raised the bar in their expectations of government and corporate leadership in times of crisis and turbulence, and so it is worth sharing some perspective of events that occurred during the global pandemic.

ANZAC Day, the 25th of April 2020, was a day like no other we have experienced in our country's history.

Covid-19 had swept through the world. That day, we watched the news that 52,234 people died of the virus in the United States alone and nearly 10,000 people per day were dying of the virus in the United Kingdom. At that point, about 250,000 people had died of the virus internationally – and there was no immediate end to this in sight. In the midst of the pandemic, with no vaccine in place and no certainty when one would be made available to people across the World, uncertainty ruled the day.

In Australia, we have traditionally gone out at dawn on that date and attended the solemn but proud commemoration of the sacrifice of the service men and women who have served our country over the decades in wars since the Gallipoli campaign. The Gallipoli landing of military boats in the year 1915, about 12,500 kms away, was not a military success; thousands of young Australians died on those shores on that day and in the months that followed, but what we do recognise is the sacrifice made for our freedom and wellbeing by them and indeed all those who have followed in that spirit of self-sacrifice.

ANZAC Day is somewhat unique across the world in the way the youngest generations of our nation participate in and feel very strongly about our ANZAC heritage.

On that ANZAC Day, I was very aware of how this also relates to the 'war' that raged against the Covid-19 pandemic, where at great personal risk, doctors, nurses, ambulance, and emergency services workers put their lives on the line to help those afflicted. The ANZAC veterans were amongst the most vulnerable to the impacts of the virus that took such a toll on the elderly of our global community.

While every death and serious illness is a sad occurrence, compared to other nations, Australia was 'lightly' touched to that date by the virus. Just 6,687 cases of Covid-19 had been confirmed in Australia, and 78 deaths in Australia associated with the virus since it arrived on our shores.

In Western Australia, there had been 548 confirmed cases and 8 deaths. In the Mid-West region where we live, there had been 8 recorded cases and no deaths up to that time.

Why did the State of Western Australia and our nation do so well in reducing the Covid-19 impact on our people compared to others?

For one, our island nation is somewhat isolated from other major centres of the pandemic, although we are also very much part of the global community. Thousands of people were travelling to/from Australia to all those countries as the pandemic emerged, so it is not just the geographic distance that saved us.

We had some very sensible and mature leadership emerge at a political level. While the politicians did struggle with the enormity of the threat and what was required to best prevent its spread in the early stage, particularly in how to meet the health challenges while trying to minimise the social and economic disruption, they did a fairly good job. This contrasts significantly to what seems to have occurred in several other countries.

In the United States, political imperatives were not fully aligned with the best interests of the country's community. Some Americans were deliberately flouting the regulated health restrictions and turning out with semi-automatic weapons (can you believe that) in great numbers at large protests. Proudly waving United States' flags and banners in throngs, they protested their freedom to work – regardless of the health threat to their own families and fellow Americans. In fairness, there were reasons; there is a large proportion of people in that country suffering financially due to the lack of work and their low levels of income, so many were feeling the burden heavily.

An estimated 60% of North Americans supported the continuation of the health restrictions, as they should, as about 30,000 people per day were dying of the virus while the protests against the restrictions were occurring. It was a very, very sad contradiction of views, priorities and values of the people of one nation.

It was not helped by the failure of political leadership at a time when government needed to guide the country clearly and unambiguously through the crisis. History showed further major escalation of the virus outbreak and many more thousands lost their lives.

In fact, there seems to be a correlation between a disconnect in political leadership required to meet the challenge and how the virus impacted various countries across the world. While these nations have paid a toll in both loss of life and economic impact, it can also be said that it revealed much about an inherent lack of just and caring leadership that some countries have in place.

The virus developed in China, and this in itself was a situation that was likely unavoidable, however the condemnation by many nations was fierce. It was directed at how China state purportedly suppressed the concerns raised by their own medics about the severity of the illness the virus created and its effects. The political system and lack of communication resulted in delays in appropriate response, allowing the virus to spread, with devastating impact on the city of Wuhan and in time across the World. The lack of transparency displayed by that country also resulted in a lack of international confidence in the information that came from them on the issue.

In the United Kingdom, some poor government decision-making saw the massive escalation of cases with an approach classed as 'let it rip' by other countries. They became the highest effected country in Europe, and it was distressingly common to see doctors and nurses going online to plead for people to stay home and observe 'social distancing' and good hygiene. Many medical staff became casualties themselves, partly due to the lack of adequate masks, face shields, ventilators and protective equipment. The UK subsequently changed their approach, but not early enough to save their Prime Minister from contracting the virus and going through intensive care himself to survive the illness.

5th **January 2021**. The World Health Organisation reports over 4 million Covid-19 cases and 76,000 deaths were recorded over the week, bringing the cumulative cases to over 83 million and over 1.8 million deaths due to the virus up to that date. On that day, the UK had 60,916 new cases and 830 deaths (totalling 2.8 million cases and 77,346 deaths) and still escalating due to a new more transmissible mutation of the virus.

It had been a long year, shaped in many ways by how we and our governments battled with the Coronavirus. Sadly, while vaccines were just starting to be distributed in some of the hardest hit nations, the spread of the virus massively escalated.

Not only had the failure to manage the spread resulted in so many more deaths, the increased presence of the virus that was allowed to build up became a major factor in allowing more transmissible mutations to develop. A new highly-transmissible mutation escalated cases in the UK and spread to other countries, including Western Australia. Here is an example of how putting economic parameters before the well-being of people, as reflected in *let it rip* thinking of some countries' leadership, can result in escalating chaos.

The situation put the whole of the UK into lockdown for several weeks; people could only leave their homes under the strictest of conditions. The economy that was supposed to benefit from letting people move about – with largely voluntary self-managed preventions – was brought to a standstill.

In Australia we had not been untouched, but in contrast our total cases to 6ᵗʰ January 2021 totalled 28,536, with 909 deaths. Lockdowns were placed in suburbs of Sydney and strict controls existed there and in Victoria to bring outbreaks under control. State governments were being very careful in regulating access/travel between States and the government of Western Australia was consistently very conservative in letting anyone in. However, our WA economy did very well overall and its exports, particularly of iron ore, provided a strong contribution to the entire nation in extremely difficult global economic circumstances.

At our home State, successful containment of the virus meant we enjoyed near total freedom, with shopping, events, tourism throughout the State, and business operations virtually as normal, largely through keeping the virus out and mandating health controls.

Internationally, we witnessed some amazing transformations in the environment around major cities. Rivers such as the Ganges in India, which has been polluted to devastating levels (even though it supplies drinking water to 400 million people), was flowing clean; people were seeing blue skies and scenery for many kilometres in cities around China that have experienced decades of grey, pollution laden atmosphere. What we were seeing and having greater appreciation of are just small glimmers of what our earth's environment could be if it were better cared for.

Private enterprise responded to the circumstances in many different ways.

Cruise ships were the source of many early cases, especially in Australia, with trips still departing full of people, even when the devastating effects of the virus were already known. Their lack of reporting of cases, release of potentially infected people from their ships, and potential misrepresentation of the level of on-board infection were matters of investigation. The actions of health authorities in respect to a vessel known as the Ruby Princess were also investigated for their lack of implementing appropriate controls, with that ship allowed to berth into Sydney. The release of infected passengers resulted in about 10% of the total cases and deaths through the virus in Australia in the immediate months that followed.

Others, though, really stepped up. Our banks, for example, extended opportunities to defer mortgage payments on loans to people who were in difficult financial circumstances, property owners were reducing rents where circumstances allowed, companies with work expanded opportunities for employment to those needing jobs, and airlines offered returning flights to Australians stranded in other countries.

The change displayed by the major banks in offering mortgage support to their customers during the time of the pandemic was particularly interesting. The earlier major Royal Commission into the financial sector revealed disgraceful behaviour, such as charging fees to deceased people, overcharging and a range of similar deceptions, resulting from sick and distorted organisational cultures and practices. They were clearly the royal commission investigations we needed to have!

The Australian Government also formed a national cabinet of State Premiers with the Prime Minister as the major decision-making body to tackle the Covid-19 challenges. This worked effectively, particularly in the crucial early stages. Opposition parties also worked with the elected State and Commonwealth parties in a collaborative way, serving the national interest. However, things slowly slid back to the status quo, particularly as the worst of the crisis began to pass; States did more and more of their own thing, each started criticising steps other States took, and the bi-partisan approach between the major parties steadily dissolved.

These are just some circumstances and examples of events of this time to assist understanding, not all. Also, these examples serve to emphasise that governments can get it wrong and should not be seen as the means to address all social, environmental, or economic challenges.

Clearly, governments at all levels and politicians across parties can collaborate in the national interest when its citizens face crises. Beyond this too was the enormous collaborative international effort to develop and distribute lifesaving vaccines. As wonderful and successful as these joint efforts were, however, the Coronavirus crisis also showed that giving more power and responsibility to government can also lead to poor outcomes if governance, leadership, and systems are not in tune with the community and the realities to be faced.

But the actions of political leaders are also a lot about what we demand of them, and the environment created by the media. They are as much trapped into behaviours and the politics of the system as we are.

Maybe we would have better nations if we allowed politicians to occasionally make a mistake:

- *They could change their approach if a better way was found.*
- *We would have less distortions of truth and facts.*
- *They could say sorry and commit to righting wrongs.*

None of these can be done if they are never allowed to get it wrong.

We all need to make mistakes, partly so we retain humility, partly so we learn and grow. We can then make better decisions and become better leaders and people.

9

Dear Rose

When you feel truly happy, stop for a moment and consider deeply what is giving contentment and enjoy that, but also reflect and seek more in your life of what you have found.

Dear Rose Faith, what a wonderful moment when you joined our happy family group on the 3rd of September 2021. And what an eventful time we had as a family and community over the weeks that followed!

It was a delight to have a brief nurse of you after your birth, but I was worried when you had to return to hospital just a week later with pneumonia. Fortunately, you fought that off. While Western Australia was relatively free of the Coronavirus, it still hung a dark shadow over us when the beautiful new addition to the family was in such a vulnerable situation with serious respiratory health challenges.

You continued to grow stronger and are now a healthy little girl surrounded by a loving family.

Your mum and dad love traditional names, and like your big sister, you have beautiful names in Rose Faith. I don't believe it is by any accident that in these challenging times 'Faith' is your middle name.

What Is Faith?

Faith comes in many forms. We put our faith in people and organisations we know and trust, like having friends pick up our children from school, accepting goods we purchase in the expectation they will be fit for purpose, assuming our employers will deliver our wages due on pay-day. This is in the knowledge that we live in an imperfect world and absolute guarantees don't exist. We blindly put our faith in others when we drive our rural highways. At the speed limit, approaching cars are coming at the combined velocity of 220 km per hour, and we assume they are fully capable of keeping to their side of the white line as we speed past, just one or two metres from them.

When we consider faith at the spiritual level, such as in connection and appreciation of others, to nature, earth, or a divine creator, it can take a whole new dimension.

> *Faith can become a special power that transcends the care and kindness we may provide others, to higher order acts of love.*

How your spiritual growth will evolve Rose, no-one can know. It will mostly be up to your choices but will be affected by the people you engage with, life events and the values you come to live by. Just be open to what is good and see how that resonates with you.

Your choice

Who we are is shaped by many things: our genetic make-up, the physical environment we experience over the journey, our family and friends and social and cultural experiences, education and work experiences, and what life dishes up.

These and more factors shape us but what defines us is our character, the ingrained values we adopt, and the choices we make.

As tiny as you are Rose, you have already faced huge challenges in your early life, and as much as I hope you and all my children and grandchildren will be untouched by some of the terrible realities that exist in our world, I know you will still face obstacles and disappointments along your life's journey.

There are many people who will provide you with love and support in your life and I want to share a story of one of the special ones. I like to think she is still looking out for you now. When just 5 days old, you got to meet your great-grandmother, Mumma. Not that you would remember this, but I have a wonderful photo of your Mumma nursing you, with a lovely smile on her face. She was in declining health due to her age but you clearly brought great pleasure to her at the time.

Our family has a strong attachment to Mumma, formed over the years. She visited us many times as your Mum, uncles and aunties were growing up, especially at Christmas time, when we went to Rottnest Island on holiday as a family, or when we needed a little help, such as the occasions when your Nanna Jill went into hospital to have a baby. She had a strong Catholic faith and lived her life accordingly. In her last days Mumma would be saying *Amen, Amen, Amen* whenever she was disturbed, woken up or confused.

Sadly, Mumma passed away on the 16th of October, not long after your birth, making it a challenging time for the family, and with your health issues too.

But that was not all that happened that day; in the early hours of that morning, a little 4-year-old girl, Chloe Smith, mysteriously disappeared from the tent she was sleeping in with her family at a camping ground at the 'Blowholes', north of Carnarvon. This is about 600 km north of where your Nanna and Papa live, and like people all over Australia, we were very concerned about that little girl's welfare. As the next few weeks passed, the police and communities across Western Australia searched for any signs or clues as to little Chloe's whereabouts, and all sorts of theories arose, but her family and community members across the State, and especially in her hometown of Carnarvon, maintained *faith* that she would be found.

Over those same weeks, members of our family sadly undertook the preparations for Mumma's commemoration mass and the wake which followed. The Covid travel restrictions were eased between Queensland and Western Australia just in time to allow some family members to get over for the event. Your Aunty Brooke travelled over a little earlier from Canberra and had to stay quarantined for two weeks, but the timing worked for her too. Only your Uncle Jason was prevented due to the higher levels of Covid cases in New South Wales, but he managed to attend via video link.

You were well recovered from your illness, so everyone was so happy to see you at Mumma's wake. Many of the extended family met you for the first time and were delighted with your beautiful and generously shared smiles.

Mumma's funeral mass was held on Wednesday, 3rd November 2021, and it was a very meaningful service in which many of the family participated in differing ways to respect and celebrate the life of that wonderful lady who meant so much to us all.

A small *miracle* occurred that day. A full eighteen days after her disappearance and when most of the broader community had given up all hope, Chloe Smith was recovered by police, alive and healthy, in the early hours of that morning.

There has been a strong link between your Mumma and young children in particular; we saw it in how she supported and shared in the life of our growing family. She was universally loved by all her children, grandchildren and great grandchildren. I made comment at her wake to a couple of family members in jest, that Mumma did not waste any time once she got to heaven in advocating and making sure that you Rose got healthy and well, and that young Chloe was also protected until she was found.

A bit of humour, coincidence, colourful thinking, or divine intervention; people with different ways of thinking will see the above events in various ways. For me, I first saw it all as coincidence until I thought about Mumma and her beliefs. I considered that if I do believe in the power of prayer and benefits of heavenly advocacy, then why would I not believe that Mumma, with her love of family and children, would not have acted to play a part, whether it be big or small?

Faith, in my experience, is found through being open to and looking for the spiritual elements of our everyday lives, and in appreciation of the gifts of life and creation. So, I hope in your life's journey little Rose Faith that you look and find your belief, and it brings you hope and great joy, as I wish for all our family and children of the world.

> *"Some people, in order to discover God, read books.*
> *But there is a great book:*
> *The very appearance of created things.*
> *Look above you! Look below you! Note it. Read it.*
> *God, whom you want to discover, never wrote that book in ink. Instead,*
> *he set before your eyes the things he made.*
> *Can you ask for a louder voice than that?"*
> *- St Augustine of Hippo (354 - 430)*

Children, like Chloe Smith, are vulnerable to threats that were unheard of when my generation grew up, when people did not even lock their cars or front doors.

My sincere hope for our grandchildren and for children to come is a place where you can truly enjoy the beauty of the environment we live in and exist in a safe and just society. This is why advocacy for Global Balance in economics, society and environment is important in taking us forward.

The challenges I have faced in my life have been tempered by what I believe in. I encourage you, Rose, to seek to discover what creation and your existence in the wonderful, infinite universe means to you.

This all flows to our spiritual, physical, and mental well-being and purpose in life. It helps us cope with all sorts of challenges, shapes our interactions with others and the Values we need to be true to, providing balance and joy in life.

It seems that those people who have spiritual beliefs that value and respect others are the ones happiest in their own lives. They are the ones best able to cope and respond with courage when things get tough.

> *Some do not feel the love that is given in this World;*
> *But if they choose not to see it, then sure, it will seem as if it doesn't*
> *exist, for them.*

Across the globe, people's lives have been affected by the recent major disasters of the world: bushfires destroying millions of hectares of country, taking lives and destroying property; the impacts and deaths across the world due to Coronavirus; but just as prevalent, the deterioration of the planet's environment caused by climate change impacts.

Climate Change is a major concern because if it continues to escalate, the negative effects on your generation's lives, and those of future children, will go on for decades.

My spiritual beliefs have helped me find strength and to see greater purpose. It has helped also to restore some faith at times when I lost belief in the basic decency of mankind. It is not just the pursuit of financial benefit while disregarding the impacts on the physical place we live in that I found wearying at times, but also the way people have treated one another and how we as societies can simply ignore the plight of others.

World events in early 2022 were dominated by the Russian invasion of Ukraine, which saw mass relocation of millions from their homes, targeting and deaths of citizens, including children and the hospitalised. There was a growing level of international anger at the tactics employed against a smaller nation. People worldwide empathise with the Ukrainian families and community. We have been in wonder at how valiantly they have met the challenge.

We are inundated and overwhelmed at times with bad news: Covid-19, floods, heat waves, fires and famines (due to advancing climate change), ethical failures of political and industry leaders, tsunamis and wars, such as the Ukraine conflict. And always it is the innocent and vulnerable that suffer most! In our part of regional Australia, despite our relative prosperity, youth suicide and decline in mental health are escalating problems. The challenge today is to maintain hope and faith in a positive future, even when bad news and devastating events dominate.

With continuation of current trends, I am deeply concerned for your future, but I can also see some good that so often emerges in these situations.

- In the eastern states of Australia, massive flooding occurred in 2022, destroying thousands of homes and claiming lives, with reported 1-in-500 year floods in some towns/cities, but the Australian community rallied with support and funding and so many heroic stories emerged of how everyday people stepped up to help those affected.

- Russian people themselves are risking retribution from their government to protest and speak out against the invasion of Ukraine. A wonderful example is a young woman, an editor in a national Russian television network, who walked onto a live news broadcast with a placard denouncing the invasion and saying to the Russian people they are being fed lies. There are so many examples of decency and compassion being extended to Ukrainian people, from neighbouring European countries' people opening their homes to the displaced, providing transport and all forms of assistance, to the donations and huge mobilisation of aid from countries and humanitarian organisations worldwide.

- More and more major companies and countries are moving to net zero targets, renewables and low emissions' technologies in concert with growing expectations of community. At the same time, new technologies are being developed to facilitate the necessary changes so that the economic advantages are swinging even more powerfully to adopting environmentally responsible ways forward over the traditional high emissions technologies.
- Higher vaccination levels and new medical treatments reduced the death rates and hospitalisation of people suffering COVID-19.

There is a long way to go, but every disaster seems to also provide a new opportunity to display the enormous potential of human decency and spirit in the face of adversity. There is the opportunity for international communities and their leaders to learn the value of groups engaging in respectful dialogue and common efforts to achieve mutual good.

Don't underestimate the Value of doing good things for nothing more than the satisfaction and privilege of giving a hand.

The world has seen unimaginably bad events in the past, with 50 million people dying of the 'Black Death' in the 14th century, an incredible 60% of Europe's population! In the first half of the 20th century, they experienced World War I, an influenza epidemic, the Great Depression and World War II followed, bringing decades of oppression to people's lives. However, the presence of nuclear threats and potential of devastation through climate change are unprecedented in the existential threat to the entirety of humanity. While the challenges we face are enormous, they are not beyond us as individuals, communities, countries, and united nations to overcome. We are all effected and must all play our part.

There are some absolutely wonderful social enterprises and charitable organisations taking on some of the world's greatest challenges. *Thankyou*[10] is a social enterprise that develops sustainable products and direct the profits towards extreme poverty, and *Charity: Water*[11] has funded over 138,000 water projects in its quest to bring clean and safe drinking water to millions in need. These are just two extraordinary examples of people coming together, creating a vision for a better world, and leading essential change.

I love what I am seeing in the way many young people think and value the world and how they respect others.

Rose, you with Sunny, Flora and Lucy are such beautiful children, and your personalities are starting to shine. Rose, your generous smiles are such a delight; Sunny, such a loving but strong, smiley little fellow, bringing happiness to all around; Flora, so full of life and adventure, which is so important for discovery, love and care of our environment; and Lucy, such an intelligent, highly capable and considerate person – all of which will be important qualities in finding sustainable and caring ways forward for our society.

You and all children will need to be strong and resilient as you face the challenges in your lives, and this will be helped if you take the time to pursue understanding of your beliefs and values.

> *We are happiest when the heart and mind are aligned. Life doesn't always allow this but if we strive to do so, our lives are so much more purposeful and joyful.*

10

Sister Spirit

Spreading goodwill, treading lightly on the sand,
Sowing seeds of growth with gentle caress of hand.

Her smile ignites the hearts of people everywhere,
Connecting with their being, in a manner tender and rare.

She was there in the beginning, witnessing all that took place;
She will be there in the end, sharing her guiding grace.

Clothed in shimmering turquoise of the sunlit morning sea,
As she goes on her mission of solace for you and me.

As humankind emerged early in birth,
She taught nature's ways, and they called her Mother Earth.

She has been part of the journey each and every day,
With her lantern of gentle love to light the true way.

Reaching out to many as she seeks to share,
With those who desperately need her love, guidance and care.

People facing war, famine and doom,
Find her close to their hearts,
If they just make room.

Terrible acts inflicted on innocents leaves her forlorn;
Earth shakes as she trembles; it's for them she does mourn.

Her heart breaks as she bears unquenchable pain;
Her tears take form as the flooding rain.

As fish choke on plastics do you think she would not care?
Just sit there, dormant, as birds fall from the air?

Oh, fools who think you can put profit first,
Can you only learn through hunger and thirst?

For all the neglect, there is a price to pay,
But beauty and love can still win the day.

There is still time, fate is not sealed,
With grace and kindness, the way is revealed.

Pause politics and industry; take time to reflect.
Put away weapons, prejudices and moral defect.

Just as the purifying waters fall to cleanse Earth,
Unite to free nature, sky, and land of the curse.

Regardless though of the path that each takes,
Have faith she shares the journey, despite the mistakes.

The spiritual sister of God's children from the start,
The sum of all that is love in every human heart.

11

Sunrise: Sunset

Our differences in belief lead to differences in thinking, which is central to creativity. Let's celebrate our diversity, thrive and reach new heights!

Our dear children are at the Sunrise of life; I am at the Sunset.

We all shine; children with the beauty and promise that their youth offers to the world, and people of my age with the knowledge and life's learnings that we are happy to share in our care for family, others, and this earthly place.

As a child grows, so many choices open in how to live their life, make earnings to provide for themselves and others, and the way they may walk the earth; in fact, how they develop into the whole person they are destined to be.

We all have different paths to walk, and each has a purpose in life to fulfill. We should seek enlightenment all along life's journey. Let's treasure the precious gift of life we have been given and that which has been given to all life that exists in the universe.

While I have suggested that solving the problems of our world can be assisted by taking a lunar viewpoint, being the most amazing person one can be is going to need an even greater leap in perspective. A leap toward our existence in an infinite universe; one which we have only the most rudimentary understanding of.

Like many, I believe in the purpose of life and creation, which extends way beyond the physical, time-bound perception that I am capable of building through what I see, experience and can conceive.

I don't believe that science will ever disprove the existence of the spiritual. That way of thinking in my mind is just a self-imposed limitation of what exists. While I have my own spiritual beliefs, it is not my intention to tell you what you should believe, rather to encourage you to be open and to pursue your beliefs through reflection.

In my faith journey, an appreciation of the beauty and miracle of the universe and the good within humanity, has deepened my appreciation of creation and the Creator. I think the existence of love in this world, including the personal and special love we have between us, grandparents to grandchildren and across our family, is a spiritual reality that goes beyond physical behaviours or mental thought processes. If you want a starting point for looking at spiritual belief and growth, then Love is where I would suggest the only meaningful foundation can be established. And don't be deterred by those who say that there cannot be a god of Love because no god would permit the abominable behaviour we see in the news every day, including the poor actions of some individuals professing a belief in God.

Yes, there are unbelievable levels of evil that exist in this world, as well as unimaginable acts of kindness, love and beauty, and both exist in an environment of free will.

I know I could not be the god of this world as I could not withstand some of the persecution and ugliness inflicted by some people on others without intervening. But even if one did, then the gift of free will and self-determination of our future world would not exist. So, while I try to do my part as best I can in making the world better, I couldn't take on God's job!

Christianity and other major religions have belief in a God of Love who is reaching out to all people; that is some 8 billion people with different experiences, cultural backgrounds, intellects, and abilities. I think that is why so many different religions and beliefs (or non-beliefs) exist, as every single individual now and throughout the existence of humankind is offered a personal invitation to a loving relationship that is unique to them. I would not be surprised when those who accept that invitation discover at some future moment that believers of this love find they were all engaged with the same loving god... and the differences each culture has created in beliefs just fall away. I think we will find we have a woefully limited understanding of the true god – just as well God is of love and forgiveness!

A few realisations that I also wish to share follow.

One thing I would have done differently is to develop an understanding of and to pursue 'mindfulness' far earlier in my adult life. Understanding my own thought processes, opening myself more to consideration of people and the place we exist in, seeking self-improvement and growth are just some of the benefits that would have significantly aided my life's journey. Since starting along this path in the past year or so, I sleep better, have improved capacity to withstand the stresses and strains of life, feel a greater sense of self-value and have grown a deeper appreciation of the beauty of creation. It complements all of the other elements of my life that contribute to my physical, mental and spiritual well-being.

> *"Exercise gives us health of the body; meditation gives us health of the mind. Each strengthens the other." - Tamara Levitt, CALM*

I've found mindfulness and meditation a great antidote to stress and it has helped my perspective of life. I found an appreciation of all that exists in my world experience. I had a great sense of that following a recent dream, which was related to something that actually happened to me in my twenties that I would like to share with you.

Early in my career, I was an engineer employed by the Main Roads Department in Bunbury. I loved my work, with responsibility for building roads and bridges across the South-West region of Western Australia. I was just married and together we had our whole life ahead of us. I was also physically fit, enjoying running, swimming, squash and diving. So, life was good, with a world of opportunities ahead.

Strangely, my dream recalled the event of 40 years ago when I had a (benign) lump removed from the back of my neck. A fairly routine surgery to be undertaken by my regular doctor at a hospital, but with the lump being right near the spine it carried some potential risk. The risk of anything going wrong was extremely low and not something I gave any real consideration to, even though the consequences could have been paralysis or even death I guess, given the operation was on the neck.

I had a local anaesthetic, so while I couldn't see what was happening, I was conscious of the whole procedure.

I seem to recall the doctor had a bit of a shake in his hand but didn't put any significant concern to that as everything done up to the point of starting the procedure was all very professional and I was quite relaxed about having it undertaken.

However, at that point the doctor took the scalpel and before even touching me he accidentally made a deep slice into a finger on his other hand (presumably holding my neck, as he was about to start). The attending nurse seemed horrified and acted quickly to firstly deal with what must have been a nasty gash on his finger and then to bring in another doctor who took over the situation, helped with the doctor's hand, and then undertook the procedure on my neck.

Obviously, I wasn't happy with the situation but never really gave it a lot of thought afterward. I subsequently heard a rumour the doctor in question had a drinking problem and left General Practice sometime later, but I couldn't verify that.

Why, though, would I have a vivid dream about that particular event that happened some four decades earlier? I pondered that and realised that if there had not been some fateful or divine intervention at that time my chances of significant damage to my spine or an artery would have gone from extremely unlikely to a very real possibility.

Everything in my life over the past forty years would have been different: my career, ability to do the sports and physical activities I enjoy, and would I even have any children or my precious grandchildren?

I feel no anger towards the doctor involved, I do not know anything really about his circumstances nor even definitively if he was at fault, but what I do feel, after the realisation of what it all meant, is a deep appreciation of all that I have received in the life that I have been gifted, of family, and all those who share the journey of living a life based on common human decency.

There was also another fateful time in my early twenties, when I was part of a team that rode on horseback searching for 'skeleton weed' (a noxious weed that threatened WA's agricultural sector) along the 530 km stretch of railway line between Northam and Kalgoorlie. Towards the end of the journey, we swam the horses bare-back in a dam nearly completely full of water. It was a lot of fun until we got to the middle of the dam and my horse suddenly went berserk. I got tossed off and was hanging onto the reins just behind it. Then the horse started kicking wildly and I could feel the force of the water as its rear hooves thrashed back and forth just centimetres from my chest. I still don't know how I avoided getting my chest stoved in on that day!

It wasn't the horse's fault. For some reason there was a section of barbed-wire fence hidden below the water surface across the middle of the dam; the poor horse was cut quite badly and had to be treated and taken back to its owner's farm as soon as that could be arranged.

People do experience all kinds of events and threats in their lives and most often come out of them with close escapes. There are many other events that I could also share that indicate a 'charmed' life, from being trapped in a small tunnel while scuba diving, swimming kilometres across a harbour known for large, finned predators, snorkelling within 150 metres of a White Pointer shark; on reflection, keeping my 'guardian angel' busy it seems. Stories for another day perhaps.

Embracing mindfulness and seeking enlightenment in whatever positive form that may take is what I would recommend as a fundamental part of life. With the challenges facing us and future generations now, balanced thinking and good mental health will be so important to life decisions and well-being.

When it comes to *faith,* perhaps consider this – do you feel, see or experience love as something more than just a way of thinking or physical sensation? If so, I suggest it must have a spiritual essence and presence. This takes us beyond our physical environment and presumably is not bound by time. Love is widely considered the greatest of all gifts, the foundation of the world's great religions and something that makes us 'whole'. I know that I love all my grandchildren, and if able will continue to do so following my passing from this earthly existence, as would others, including mums and dads, family before us and family to follow.

> *"We are like islands in the sea, separate on the surface but connected in the deep." - William James*

12

Around, Over & Through

Given the choice, always choose to work with the environment – not in defiance, ignorance or arrogance of the forces of nature.

As we move to a world in which severe and increasingly unpredictable extreme events are more regularly experienced across the globe, is it a time to rethink how we construct and retain our homes, cities and major infrastructure that connects and provides for our communities?

In years gone by, working respectfully with the natural landscape was front and centre in building and infrastructure construction. This was in part due to limited financial and deployable resources, more limited technology, and knowledge. However, in many instances the quality and longevity of buildings, roadways and infrastructure built in earlier eras exceeds that of today.

How many of us would just love to have had the finances to afford to purchase some of the magnificent heritage homes where these have been retained, with their outstanding architectural features, high ceilings and verandas.

I was fortunate to grow up in an area of renown natural beauty, at Exmouth, on the doorstep of the magnificent world heritage-listed Ningaloo Coast. As a cyclone prone area, a respect for the incredible forces of nature was instilled within our community.

Later, as a civil engineer, my deep respect for the forces of nature continued to grow, especially when I had to design and construct massive drainage systems in the Kimberley region. I saw firsthand just how unforgiving nature can be in pounding structures and infrastructure that was not built in harmony with its ways.

I will never forget the time in 1988, I was travelling from our home in Broome up to Derby to visit friends for a weekend of playing squash. As part of its Bicentennial national infrastructure development program, the Commonwealth Government had just built what was intended to be an all-weather highway over the flood-prone lands adjacent to the Fitzroy River crossing between Broome and Derby. As the Shire Engineer in Broome, I had a real interest in the massive scale of the works, with kilometres of huge, elevated roadway, protected with rocks, metres in diameter, and rock-filled mesh 'mattresses' that weighed tonnes. Following completion of this significant engineering feat, a major storm system hit the area, with significant flooding within the expansive Fitzroy River catchment, and I was keen to see how the nationally significant roadworks project stood up.

As I drove past a large Bicentennial roadworks sign, proudly erected by the government, I was staggered by the flood's impact. The torrential waters had carved through road embankments that stood 10 to 15 metres high, with utter disregard. As I continued along a temporary detour constructed through one damaged section, I had the strange experience of looking up at a 15 metre-high bridge structure standing in isolation. Like a lone pylon, it had no connection left to the remaining road embankments! Further along there were several large washouts, protective rock mattresses weighing tonnes had been picked up and could now be seen wrapped around trees, hundreds of metres downstream.

I contacted Main Roads after the trip and suggested they may want to quietly remove the signs advertising the bi-centennial achievement.

Some years later, as a consulting engineer, I faced the challenges of the mighty Fitzroy River myself in helping to guide the earthworks, road and drainage design of the Fitzroy River Lodge. This was a resort development being built adjacent to the river, just out of Fitzroy Crossing townsite. By that time in my career, I had learnt a lot of lessons that were never part of a university course, particularly when it came to working with Kimberley soils. Those soils were rock hard when dry but melt like butter when exposed to the torrential rains that were such a dominating factor in WA's top-end.

A commitment I made to any engineering project I was engaged in was to walk every section of road or drain that I designed, to ensure I had a first-hand appreciation of the physical environment. When putting this into practice at the planned resort site, walking adjacent to the banks of the mighty Fitzroy River, I was gobsmacked to see white paint marks several metres up on the passing power poles. Later, I learnt that these were put there by government workers, operating from a dingy at the peak of a recent large flood event – metres higher than the planned resort site.

Our company's advice to the client was simple – don't build there! However, they were insistent that they understood the risks, were going to proceed, and the client not only lived in the region but had a lot of practical skills and knowledge to draw on.

The project proceeded and our company gave him the most practical solutions we could in order to achieve the resort project. The major buildings were set on huge earth mounds designed at heights above the adjacent Fitzroy River Bridge. These had gentle slopes, covered with a layer of concrete blanket protection and then topped with topsoil, grassed and planted out. Access roads and paths were set near ground level to minimise any impediment to natural floodwater flow, designed with gentle gradients and to act as drains themselves as water levels dropped. Even the sewerage systems were designed to be capped off to seal out floodwaters in major storm events. Importantly, a preparation and evacuation plan was drawn up for any major flood event; evacuation was quite achievable as reasonable advance notice of major flood levels is available from upstream monitoring.

Practical designs were also used, like putting accommodation units up on steel-framed stilts designed to take the forces of floodwater and waterborne debris, creating the extra benefit of shaded carparking below for year-round use.

Yet another massive 1-in-100 year flood recently thumped the town of Fitzroy Crossing and saw the very bridge referred to above destroyed, with the Fitzroy River Lodge becoming the base for emergency services and contractors. The new widened bridge, built to higher and stronger standards, has just been opened, and the Fitzroy River Resort proudly sits by on the eastern riverbank.

I am not suggesting that we do not need to build structures that are designed to stand up against the highest orders of nature's forces. Rather, that design which conforms to the natural flows of wind, stormwaters, earth movement and perhaps fires, rather than straight-up defiant barriers to these movements, may in many cases be a more affordable and practical approach to the escalation in magnitude and frequency of disastrous weather events. In appropriate situations, allowing the forces of nature to flow around, over or through may be the best long-term option!

Just a few decades ago, it was not uncommon to have even major highways and roads closed for days at a time in flood-prone or cyclonic areas, and communities lived with this. (Some still do). In earlier times, our governments did not have the resources to build the flood-proof roadways that are now the general expectation and basically the only option then was lower level, lower impact construction. Perhaps more design and research in strengthening lower impact, designed roadways and structures is justified.

Several years ago, I wrote to the State Premier's Office suggesting that given the expectation of increased cyclone severity and their tracking further south (predicted due to climate change), it would be prudent for the State to work with the Institution of Engineers Australia on wind-hardy buildings. In particular, they should review wind design and building standards for residences in more southern areas of Western Australia. Obviously not an immediate solution, but this would lead over time to more and more houses being built to a standard that could reasonably stand up to the increased storm impacts predicted. Nothing came of that suggestion at the time.

On 11th April 2021, Category 3 Cyclone Seroja crossed the Western Australian coast between Geraldton and Kalbarri. It was a frightening experience sitting in our house in Geraldton as the winds peaked that evening. But it was devastating for the people of Kalbarri and several inland communities that experienced their homes, farm buildings and businesses being destroyed around them.

Processes are underway to implement new and improved building standards, and while this is a good thing, the fact that so little has been put in place despite over 20 years of awareness of the threat of climate change, means we now need major action. All levels of government and industry need to put major research, design and development effort into modification of existing buildings as a matter of urgency. This is particularly in the case of wind, flood and fire protection, including cost effective measures that can be implemented by government, business and homeowners.

When you think about this increase in climatic disasters, it seems like Mother Earth has tried in many ways to coerce mankind into being kinder in our worldly existence:

- Disease has had global impacts on the world's population
- Warming has impacted the natural beauty we value and taken an increasing number of plant and animal species to extinction
- Storms have driven floods, cyclones and tornadoes across the lands
- Heat and drying climate has devastated crops, bushland and led to widespread famine
- Storm waves and king tides eat away at our beaches
- Rising water levels submerge islands and low lying coastlines

As time passes, the extent of effort needed to protect ourselves, community, country and the world we live in from the significant consequences of environmentally generated devastation grows in magnitude.

Our future well-being is no longer assured just by reducing greenhouse emissions and other forms of environmental degradation alone.

That opportunity has passed!

13

Imagineering

Imagineering is found at the convergence of creativity, science, engineering and technology, and requires emotional intelligence. It is not about fantasy but applying creative thought, imagination, and empathy to design, technology, and development. As the world adopts more and more technology, with artificial intelligence and robotics taking greater control of work and daily processes, it is human creativity that will be our most important capability in future careers.

Imagination and empathy fused into new technologies opens up endless new possibilities, both for us and our communities. Its success in delivering better outcomes for society comes from infusing emotional intelligence into the design and engineering processes. This means not just understanding how people will respond to a new product, infrastructure or process at the physical level but also how they will feel and what it may do to improve quality of life, beauty of place and well-being.

Imagine... you have come back in life as a ray of light, cruising through the universe from the instant the Big Bang generated you, at a comfortable 300,000 km per second. You have been travelling for 13.7 billion years and have seen stars, planets and nebulae created and die, escaped the gravitational pull of massive black holes and now at Earth, seen the existence of life advanced to a level unseen along the entirety of this phenomenal journey. Can you wonder at what has had to have occurred here for this amazing life-sustaining planet to have come into existence? Life so fragile in such a vast and harsh universe, with such extreme forces of energy and gravitation that predominantly exist wherever else you have seen stars or planets formed.

And as you streak through the Earth's moist atmosphere an amazing thing happens, a whole new dimension of your being is revealed as the prismatic effect sees you split into glorious colours from reds, yellow, blues, through to violet and beyond to countless forms with frequencies that the eyes of those of the Earth cannot see. With that, realisation that each of those newly revealed light forms are made up of further sub elements, forces and effects, still unknown to you. That you exist in a universe that is not empty, but full, and that infinity does not just exist across the extent of the universe, it also exists within.

... Or you are a drop of water, made of pure molecules from hydrogen and oxygen, moving through the cycles of nature and mankind, sustaining life in the plants and animals you pass through, swirling through oceans and rivers, being lifted into the sky to amazing heights and then falling to the welcoming lands below. You are part of an endless and

life-giving cycle and as you pass from one part of that cycle to the next a whole new purpose for your being comes into play.

Opening up our perspective and engaging in creative activities like this can unleash new possibilities. It allows us to question and explore concepts that our minds would not contemplate if bound to fixed precepts. And we can go even further by engaging in the emotional experience of customers or affected sectors of community, by considering the flow-on outcomes to mental, physical and spiritual health, transcending those of traditional business practice or technology development. Social connection and building of community are engineered into the outcomes, rather than afterthoughts. This avoids reactivity; companies rolling out crisis management strategies to convince us that their products or practices are not as bad as we all may think!

If we start with ideas we can only dream of and then bring this perspective to our current realities, new, previously unimaginable opportunities may be revealed.

In life, many assume the spiritual and the physical are not interconnected. My career has largely been about applying science and management principles to deliver outcomes for the communities in which I have lived, but a technical orientation does not stop me from believing in the power of love and beauty. The love and beauty I have experienced, and the very existence of my children and grandchildren, are fundamental demonstrations of how our worldly existence transcends the physical.

What may be just some outcomes of the creative approach of *Renaissance 2.0* in our everyday lives?

Our towns and cities would be greener, and I don't just mean that more of what we do is powered through renewable energy (as critical as that is), but literally more **green.** Homes and apartment blocks with spaces for trees, playgrounds, gardens and communion with nature and each other.

The structure of towns intertwined with swathes of natural bush and trickling streams, wetlands, and other natural features would be carefully planned, developed and managed. Perhaps the green of our city fringes then take on a tawny tinge as they merge into valued and protected natural bushland.

And with the deliberate revegetation of the urban landscape and the expansion of tree-canopy, green tracts displace hard paving and we get to enjoy cooler city environments.

The food we eat would be travelling just metres from home gardens or perhaps a few kilometres from local horticultural and farming enterprises on the outskirts of our cities.

Local business and employment opportunities would expand, increasing the self-sufficiency of our cities and towns.

With greater emphasis on social support, regional towns and cities would boom, and have the health, educational and social services they need to reasonably support their community members from cradle to grave.

Native seeds, vegetables and fruits take a bigger part of our diet.

Our resilience in the face of natural disasters would strengthen as we adapt design and development to conform with the ebb and flow of the forces of nature.

Civic pride would be celebrated in local community centres, where we congregate to eat, work, and enjoy art, recreation and each other's company. Culture and diversity will be celebrated.

Large corporations working on how they can best integrate their operations into local communities and build their relationships with their customer base.

Further development and utilisation of renewable energy, re-use and re-purposing of materials and articles we formerly discarded; cleaner industrial processes; accelerated transition from carbon-emitting energy and technologies, bringing net zero emissions goals within reach. Even moving beyond this, to net reductions that give us the clear, clean air, waterways and seas we desire.

Elevation of importance of people-focus, emotional intelligence and skill-sets related to community building, health, social welfare, education and environment.

People passionately engaging in their chosen careers, harnessing new technologies which expand creative expression and innovation.

Creatives using augmented reality, user-perspective videos, and gaming, bringing emotion, feeling and empathy so that designers and corporate managers virtually experience the journey their clients, customers or affected communities go through as a result of new innovations, business systems or projects.

Partnerships between community based and not-for-profit organisations with corporations seeking to re-align their resources and capabilities with company sustainability objectives.

Transformation of poverty-stricken communities, built upon local resources, skills, culture, resilience and education.

Decline in bushfires and extreme weather events, consequential social impacts and displacement; stabilisation of polar ice, re-growth of forests and coral reefs; reduced pollution of our air, land and seas; humanity in harmonious *Global Balance* with Mother Earth.

In time, a new legacy of magnificent artworks, architectural structures and cities that can be celebrated by future generations, in the spirit of the Renaissance. The same qualities of inspired leadership, creativity and appreciation of the beauty of creation... enabling society to enjoy healthy, sustainable growth and communal wellbeing.

Hope!

The thing is, we have all the resources and capabilities to make all of this and so much more possible, right now.

Epilogue

Miracle in the Backyard.

Dear Lucy, Flora, Sunny and Rose

What a glorious time we had at the beautiful Rottnest Island in the Easter School Holidays of 2024. Securing a booking at that time of year was near impossible, but after years of trying, I managed to book not one, but two chalets for us to share with your families.. right on the pristine beachfront just south of the settlement... amazing!

Finding Quokkas, swimming, building sandcastles, eating ice-creams, championing mini-golf, developing bike riding skills, and just relaxing in the safe, friendly environment – just plain endless fun!

On the first day, we got right into the spirit of holiday joy, and it was fantastic to have a visit from your great uncle and his family. They were holidaying from England and joined us for a day of beachside adventure.

However, in the early evening, as we sat at the hotel enjoying pizza and drinks before farewelling our day-tripping family visitors, a strange and bizarre series of events was unfolding at Nanna and Papa's home in Geraldton.

Your Uncle Ross, who would normally have been working away, was at the house sleeping on the lounge because he was ill. As fate would have it, this was very fortunate but also could have been life threatening for him.

As he rested, a person walked through the back of our property, down near the riverbank below and went as far as the next street. Access through that area is prevented by signs erected by the City Council and by physical brush across the old tracks that cut through the bush. The same barriers exist at our end of this stretch of the river. Whether it was the restriction of access that enraged the individual or other factors, I do not know, but he was so fiercely angry that after a hail of abuse directed at the occupants of the adjacent house, he then set the bush on fire at their fence-line. The fire quickly took hold and burnt into their property, fanned by strong, easterly winds.

There were several people at the house at the time as they had a Pilates session underway, a very fortunate occurrence as these highly capable people quickly swung into action, coming together to fight the fire and call the fire brigade. Lucky also because the homeowner had acquired a firefighting pump and water tanks to address just such a situation. Not many residential homes equip themselves to this degree, and it turned out that this was very fortunate for us too.

While that was happening, the perpetrator turned around and walked back to our property, where he found a spot concealed by the native bush and bank below our house, to set another fire. The strong winds set this ablaze and fire leapt up the bank towards our house in just a few minutes.

By good fortune, a neighbour across the road saw the smoke from the first fire and then the early stage of smoke rising from the bush nearby.

Despite having had surgery for knee replacements in both legs just weeks before, he hobbled across the road and banged on our door, awakening and warning Ross of the fire. Our neighbours also rang the fire brigade, who had their teams already on the way, and they alerted them to this second fire.

The first fire was extinguished by the efforts of the owners and their Pilates friends before the fire trucks arrived, which meant that they could divert all their efforts to the fire threatening our house.

Lucky indeed because it was far more intense. While every career fire-fighter in the town battled the blaze, it burnt fences, destroyed plants and reticulation, and reached a large palm tree that sits just a metre from the wooden patio of the house. If the patio ignited, the chances of saving the house and several houses behind would have been slim indeed.

Because the fire brigade had been called earlier for the first fire, with the one below our house being lit about 10 minutes later than the first, the fire teams were at our location within about 5 minutes of it being lit. If these events did not happen in that way, our house would never have been saved. The 15 or so minutes from calling to getting to our house would have been about 10 minutes too late to save it!

We are very grateful for all the support that came to assist that day, the firefighters and police and our neighbours. Even a young fellow riding past on his bike jumped in, grabbed a garden hose, and helped your Uncle Ross to do what they could before the fire crews arrived.

Was it just a series of fortunate occurrences that saved our home and potentially Ross's life that day?

- Ross was home rather than at work – that was lucky!
- The other fire was lit first and was extinguished, freeing the fire crews up – lucky for us!
- The fire crews were already on their way when the one near our house was lit – lucky!
- Our neighbours were outside and spotted the danger early, giving Ross warning – lucky
- People passing by providing crucial help – lucky!
- A wind change assisted the fire-fighters – lucky!
- Fire was stopped within a couple of metres of the house – extremely lucky!

For us too, having family all around at the time and especially the heart-warming presence of you, our grandchildren, was wonderful in assisting us to personally cope with the situation. And as there was little that could be achieved in rushing back home, we spent the rest of our holiday enjoying family time, which is the real value in our lives.

For all of the above to happen as it did is a *miracle in our backyard*. If any one of the fortunate events did not align in a consecutive order, the strongest possibility is we would have lost our home at a minimum; anything beyond that is frankly too terrible to contemplate. The alleged perpetrator's antics were captured on security camera, he has been charged and will face the courts in the months ahead.

Responding to the Unwanted Event

In so many ways, these events, what has followed and how we have chosen to respond essentially summarises all that has been put forward in this book.

People choose to look at events like this in different ways. In basic objective terms it is one of an increasing number of criminal arson incidents that did significant harm, threatening lives and people's homes. Events like this can drive anger, fear, anxiety and a whole range of emotions. For some this could trigger a mental illness episode.

There has been some general community member outrage directed through social media at the suspect charged, but I really question what that achieves.

For me there is no anger. Dismay, yes, but I feel no enmity towards the person charged. Frankly, there is already enough anger, frustration and division in the community, and I have no desire to add to it. Although I wouldn't say that I forgive the person, simply because I don't know them at all or what the motivation may have been, if this is just one irrational event or one of several violent actions. I'm not sure I understand how you can forgive someone without at least some understanding of the person.

The only expectation I have of the justice system is that crimes of this nature are appropriately penalised to discourage others inclined towards similar behaviours from doing so. For the individual, my only hope is that they recognise the wrong, take the penalty as the opportunity to reform, learn and change, then re-enter the community as a constructive member of society.

Freeing ourselves from anger and anxiety is liberating and gives the opportunity to look at our situation more holistically.

The first thing we decided in response to the events was to turn the negative experience into a positive, and that practical process is underway.

We have:

- Recontoured the burnt-out block to maximise its view over the river
- Built a gravel track for access to the lower level of the lot close to the river, for emergency and recreational use
- Stabilised the denuded banks against flood
- Planned landscaping, terracing, gardens, vegetable patches and spaces to relax and enjoy it all
- Started replacing burnt and damaged fencing to a new and better standard
- Progressed fencing around our whole site to deter illegal access.

All this effort has built positive energy and confidence, pushing away the negatives that would have dominated our thoughts and actions if we had just let the criminal events overcome our thinking and responses.

Design and selection of the landscaping, fencing and plantings are respectful of the physical environment. We place a high value on the riverine flora and fauna, and plantings and fencing is intended to complement and integrate with what exists. The fences will allow floodwaters to pass through in high flood situations, the landscaping has also been done in a manner that works with the existing contours of the land, the native vegetation will be reinstated but with consideration of both the drying climate and likelihood of increased fire threat in the years ahead.

Additionally, we have consulted with the relevant Cultural Heritage Advisor and government agency to ensure that the works planned do not impact a registered Aboriginal Cultural Heritage Site that exists over the river waters adjacent and passes through a small corner of our property.

In short, we are endeavouring to put into practice all the concepts of balance, resilience, adaption, respect and stewardship of the environment, plus consideration of relevant cultural factors, and to enhance the outcomes in the process.

Though we were planning some of this work well before the fire, we are fortunate that we have a level of good health and resources to do these things: it has helped our own physical and mental well-being enormously. Unfortunately, many do not have the resilience nor the funds to similarly respond to criminal harm they have suffered. If society found the means of providing meaningful assistance to victims of crime, these people would have greater capacity to re-establish their lives.

I do not pretend that what we have gone through is anything like what so many other people have suffered. My hope is that somewhere within what has been shared here are strategies or ideas that you, or anyone, can utilise and adapt to help in adverse circumstances.

Getting a decent night's sleep was a challenge during the following weeks so I put into practice my developing meditation and mindfulness abilities, and these helped over time. Recognising how thought patterns can take you down negative paths, learning to acknowledge thoughts and emotions that do not serve your interests and positive growth, and then letting them go, are such valuable skills for personal well-being.

I have shared how we have responded, physically, emotionally, and strived for mental health in the process. I need to also share with you some of the spiritual journey, to be honest to the messages of this book and the true-life experience faced through this arson incident at our home.

This book was written and edited prior to the fire event, and I was in the process of doing all the administrative bits one needs to work through before loading up the book in a form that is suitable for self-publishing. I wanted to get this done by Easter 2024 but wasn't fixated on that deadline because lots of other family priorities existed at the time, including preparing for our wonderful Easter School Holiday together with you, my darling grandchildren.

Then Sister *Spirit* came to me. By that I mean the inspiration to include this poem with its messages, which resonated deeply. I felt the message of hope but also felt a premonition of impending disaster that I would have to see through. The messages of Sister *Spirit* are for all, but not just homogenously; it felt like they were for me at a personal level, as they may be for any individual. I am not a poet and have no experience as an author either for that matter, so neither of these tasks flow naturally for me.

So, I added Sister *Spirit* into the book, because the poem's messages are to share with you and any who care to listen, and I was ready to get onto the publishing process again. But time ran out and I didn't complete all the book preparation. Then it was holiday time, and I decided the deadline was not meant to be. We packed up, headed for Rottnest Island and of course the next day was our first full day there and the day of the fire.

The whole of our experience and response to the fire's fallout is a freshly lived summary of the messages of this whole book. They add a real context to ideas that may otherwise just read as conceptual. It would seem all the delays were meant to be!

I feel and see spiritual guidance and support in my life. It is as real and logical as looking both ways before crossing the road. For me living without the spiritual aspect would be like choosing to just watch television in black and white. So much missed and incomplete.

My wish for you is that you find and be true to your beliefs and a faith based upon love and respect of self, family, community and the Earth we share, to guide you in your journey.

We can look at life at a basic physical, material level; we can live it almost entirely as emotional experience, or we can devote our lives to spiritual purity and growth. Rightly or wrongly, I believe we should seek to harmonise all these elements if we want to be the best of who we are. And if we do not strike a balance between each then our physical, mental or spiritual health may suffer. But the right balance achieved is as unique to each of us, and each of us must find that balance for ourselves.

There are going to be far greater and more frequent climate-related disasters facing all humanity in the decades before us. Social media and politics continue to fuel division in society, and different nations continue to make massive investments in military capacity in a quest to dominate or intimidate others.

Despite this, more of us need to work towards peace and harmony across society and to live sustainably upon our planet Earth, shaking off feelings of hopelessness or indifference. It saddens me to the core when I look at the state of affairs that you, our precious grandchildren, and children across the world are inheriting.

Be resilient, be alert to mischievous and distorted influences, and seek balance in your lives. Seek guidance in your efforts to build a better society and world.

And, know that we love you – now and always.

The future we desire is not just in release of the intellectual potential of our minds, it's also in release of the unlimited potential of our hearts.

Some of the crazy family fun at Rottnest Island, Western Australia, 2024.

Appendix

The *Equation* for *Global Equity* has been proposed to facilitate understanding of the interactions between the financial, social and environmental outcomes of an entity.

Using the Accounting Equation as a model, it has the potential to drive environmental and social entrepreneurship and development, and to provide an objective, quantifiable and measurable information for accountability, regulation and governing policies.

Global Equity is equal to the Financial Equity, plus the Social Equity and the Environmental Equity of an entity.

As an equation:

Global Equity, (Eg) = Financial Equity, (Ef) + Social Equity, (Es) + Environmental Equity, (Ee)

Or Eg = Ef + Es + Ee

If expressed in terms of Assets and Liabilities, it would be:

Global Equity, (Eg) = { Economic Assets (Ac) – Economic Liabilities (Lc)}

        Plus *{Social Benefit (As) – Social Detriment (Ls)}*

        Plus *{Environmental Benefit (Ae) – Environmental Detriment,(Le)*

Or Eg = (Ac – Lc) + (As – Ls) + (Ae -Ls)

Where:

Eg = Global Equity

Ac = Economic Assets (Traditional financial assets)

Lc = Economic Liabilities (Traditional financial liabilities)

Ef = Financial Equity

As = Social Benefit

Ls = Social Detriment

Es = Social Equity

Ae = Environmental Benefit

Le = Environmental Detriment

Ee = Environmental Equity

References

1. State of the Climate, Australia's changing climate, CSIRO, 24 November 2022. https://www.csiro.au/en/research/environmental-impacts/climate-change/State-of-the-Climate

2. Somalia Food Insecurity Crisis, CARE, September 2022. https://www.care.org/our-work/disaster-response/emergencies/somalia-food-insecurity-crisis/

3. Overcoming impacts of desert locusts, drought and displacement through climate-smart agriculture practices and tools in Somaliland, Reliefweb, Source: Food and Agriculture Organisation of the United Nations, 6 January 2022. https://reliefweb.int/report/somalia/overcoming-impacts-desert-locusts-drought-and-displacement-through-climate-smart

4. Macquarie axes staff from banking and financial services division, Michelle Bowes, News.com.au, 2 November 2023. https://www.news.com.au/finance/business/banking/macquarie-axes-staff-from-banking-and-financial-services-division/news-story/0e840414e8263afd2d6733c652fa78be

5. Solving Tech Industry Purpose Problem, Derek Kennedy, Jim Hemerling, Kate Norton, and Cara Castellana Kreisman, Boston

Consulting Group, 5 June 2019. https://www.bcg.com/en-au/
publications/2019/solving-tech-industry-purpose-problem.aspx?

6. History of Ideas: The Renaissance, The School of Life, 6 November 2015. www.theschooloflife.com https://www.youtube.com/
watch?v=fI1OeMmwYjU

7. Sustainable Development Goals: The SDGS in Action, United
Nations Development Programme, 2024.
https://www.undp.org/sustainable-development-goals

8. Social Impact Measurement, Australian Social Enterprises, 2017.
https://asvb.com.au/social-impact-value/social-impact-
measurement/

9. Natural Capital Accounting: Overview, European Commission,
11 July 2022. https://environment.ec.europa.eu/topics/nature-
and-biodiversity/natural-capital-accounting_en

10. About: Our Mission, Thankyou, Founded 2008.
www.thankyou.co

11. Charity: Water, Website, 11 March 2024. www.charitywa-
ter.org

The Author

Rob Jefferies

Creative, Engaging Solutions is what Jefferies and Associates is about. Its founder and Managing Director Rob Jefferies has over four decades of experience working towards his personal motto of *Building Better Communities.*

Rob and his wife Jillian have six children: Ross, Natalie, Kym, Peta, Brooke, and Jason, and four grandchildren Lucy, Flora, Sunny and Rose; the love and strong family bonds are the inspiration sitting behind this book and are openly shared to invite readers to join the journey.

This book seeks to share some of Rob's personal and professional life lessons in the hope that it may stimulate new thinking and action towards addressing the challenges imperative to the lives of future generations, our children, and the health of our planet Earth.

Rob has lived and worked in regional communities, from Broome in the north, to Albany in the south of Western Australia, as well as in Perth, its capital city. With over half of his career spent in local government, he remains heavily invested in local community.

Practical experience as a civil engineer has been balanced with managerial roles covering a broad range of technical fields, strategic planning, project management and consulting work, and representation of business and industry bodies in CEO capacities. In addition to engineering, Rob has qualifications in business management and company directorship but regards the lessons of life as the most valuable.

Some of Rob's roles include CEO at the City of Geraldton, elected Councillor with the Geraldton-Greenough City Council, inaugural voluntary Chair of the Mid West R & D Network, of Funtavia Inc. and the Bendigo Community Bank in Geraldton, CEO and Deputy Chair roles at the Mid-West Chamber of Commerce and Industry, CEO and Deputy Chair of Geraldton Iron Ore Alliance and current Chair of Dunmarra Pty Ltd: covering a broad spread of community not for profit organisations and business activities in the areas of community banking, regional art, research and development, regional industry and local business.

Rob Jefferies and Associates Pty Ltd ABN 24 124 579 568 trades as

JEFFERIES & ASSOCIATES
Creative Engaging Solutions